ADAM SMITH GOES TO MOSCOW

A Dialogue on Radical Reform

Adam Smith Goes to Moscow

A Dialogue on Radical Reform

Walter Adams and
James W. Brock

Princeton University Press

Library of Congress Cataloging-in-Publication Data

Adams, Walter, 1922 Aug. 27–
Adam Smith goes to Moscow : a dialogue on radical reform /
Walter Adams and James W. Brock.
p. cm.
Includes index.
ISBN 0-691-03283-1
1. Europe, Eastern—Economic policy—1989– 2. Capitalism—
Europe, Eastern. 3. Former Soviet republics—Economic policy.
4. Capitalism—Former Soviet republics. I. Brock, James W.
II. Title.
HC244.A518   1993
338.947—dc20   93-16275

This book has been composed in Trump

FOR

Václav Havel

PLAYWRIGHT,
STATESMAN,
HUMANIST

It is said that a wonder-rabbi of Chelm once saw, in a vision, the destruction by fire of the study house in Lublin, fifty miles away. This remarkable event greatly enhanced his fame as a wonder-worker. Several days later a traveler from Lublin, arriving in Chelm, was greeted with expressions of sorrow and concern, not unmixed with a certain pride, by the disciples of the wonder-rabbi. "What are you talking about?" asked the traveler. "I left Lublin three days ago and the study house was standing as it always has. What kind of a wonder-rabbi is that?" "Well, well," one of the rabbi's disciples answered, "burned or not burned, it's only a detail. The wonder is he could see so far."

—Polish Folktale

It will be a long and arduous task. . . . All institutions whose past has been a majestic one contain, even in their decline, the power to delay the coming of their successors. They are, by our habituation to them, a sort of prison made intimate, and even dear, by the associations of an age-long history. Dwelling therein, to many of us, the prospect without seems vague and doubtful and hard. We weigh uneasily the price of escape from its confines; and the courage to attempt it is rare. But it is only as we make the effort that we can go forward with hope. For in no other fashion can we now add creative dignity to the human adventure.

—Harold J. Laski, *The State in Theory and Practice*

Contents

LIST OF CHARTS

THE euphoria that greeted the peaceful overthrow of Soviet hegemony in Eastern Europe, and the subsequent dismemberment of the Soviet Union itself, soon gave way to a period of confusion, uncertainty, and doubt. It soon became apparent that the transition from totalitarianism to democracy, and from a command-and-control system to a market economy, was more nettlesome than the newly liberated nations had at first supposed.

In the midst of these cataclysmic events, volunteers started to arrive from the West, offering advice and technical assistance. Teams from the International Monetary Fund (IMF) and World Bank, independent consultants and experts, gurus and mavens, as well as some chance travelers and charlatans, began to crisscross the region. Versed in economic theory and development economics—some with impressive experience in Latin America, Asia, and Africa—they brought with them blueprints to guide the transition. They offered their counsel with candor, conviction, and confidence—occasionally with a touch of arrogance. Reform of a comatose socialist economy, they argued, required radical action—an immediate and simultaneous implementation of marketization, privatization, and stabilization. Prices had to be deregulated, state enterprises had to be denationalized, and budgets had to be balanced. In this view, there was no alternative to a "bitter pill," "shock therapy," "Big Bang" approach. A chasm, it was said, could not be crossed in two leaps.

The governments of the newly liberated nations agreed that swift and comprehensive reform was imperative but were alarmed by its risks and dubious about its feasibility. They did not dispute the theoretical validity of the Big Bang approach, but they were concerned about its costs. They conceded that strong medicine was required, but they feared that an overdose might kill the patient. They expressed concern that their peoples might be unwilling to make wrenching sacrifices in the short run in return for deferred benefits that were neither visible nor palpable. They questioned whether governments committed to the stern austerity prescribed by the Big Bang theorists could hope to survive in office.

Political leaders in the liberated nations pointed to practical difficulties in implementing the Big Bang. Abandoning price control, they said, makes sense where markets are competitive, but is it the right policy for an economy honeycombed with monopolies? Balanced budgets and the elimination of subsidies are the very essence of wisdom and prudence; but how does one deal with the resulting collapse in industrial production, the massive bankruptcies of inefficient enterprises, and widespread unemployment? Privatization is clearly desirable; but how does one go about privatizing an economy more than 75 percent of whose property is in the hands of the state? How does one create a safety net to ameliorate the pain of the reforms? And how does one do all that in the midst of ethnic strife, nationalist animosities, and political gridlock? The task, they felt, required time. It called for patience and a policy of gradualism.

The confrontation between the Big Bang blueprint and the policy of gradualism is the subject of the ensuing dialogue (which, at times, may remind the reader of the Theater of the Absurd). Throughout, the emphasis is on questions rather than answers. Is the transition from a communist economy to a market economy more difficult than a transition the other way—is it easy enough to make fish stew out of an aquarium, but impossible to make an aquarium out of fish stew? Assuming agreement on grand strategy, what specific tactics are required to surmount the obstructionism of vested interests in the old order?[1] Given that communism was brought down by its institutions, and the inefficiency, corruption, and inhumanity they bred into the system, how does one create the new institutional infrastructure that is indispensable to a democratic market society?[2] Will a fragile democracy produce political gridlock that will obstruct the creation of this new institutional infrastructure? Paradoxically, does the transition to a free market economy, at least in its initial stages, require a more powerful rather than a less powerful state? Having repudiated communism, is there the insidious danger that people may perceive the market economy as yet another ideological cult or utopian dogma?[3] Finally, to what extent does the trans-

---

[1] Stephen F. Cohen, "What's Really Happening in Russia," *The Nation*, Mar. 2, 1992, 261.

[2] Leonard Silk, "Economic Scene," *New York Times*, May 29, 1992, C2.

[3] Peter Reddaway, "Russia on the Brink," *New York Review of Books* (Jan. 28, 1993): 30–35.

formation process in Eastern Europe lend perspective to the public policy debates in the West concerning such issues as deficit reduction, economic growth, job creation?

We wrote this book to highlight the economic issues and political complexities of transforming a totalitarian command-and-control system into a free market democracy—not to present an ideal blueprint for the transition. Our purpose is to stimulate thought, not to render judgment. That is the prerogative of the reader.

Walter Adams
James W. Brock

THIS is that rara avis in economics books—a drama. It is a drama composed from the imagination, but drawn from hard realities. The plot consists of the agonizing choices that must be made by the Prime Minister—the central protagonist, who must create for a nation, newly emerged from the rubble of the collapsed Soviet empire, some kind of viable economic framework. The Prime Minister's adversary and would-be guide is the Advisor, urging a course of action that if successful, will put the newly liberated nation on a trajectory of economic progress, but that if unsuccessful, could plunge it into anarchy and exhaustion.

This is not the first time that such a socioeconomic drama has been enacted in history. The transition from late feudalism into capitalism was another period of drama when ministers listened with one ear to bold plans for social reorganization, hearing in the other the mutterings of those who foresaw disaster if the plans failed—I think of what the court of Louis XV must have thought of the idea, proposed by François Quesnay, physician to Madame Pompadour, and Jacques Turgot, Contrôleur des Finances, to revitalize the stagnant French economy by levying taxes on the rich nobles who were the receivers of all land rents.

But never, I think, have the options been so dramatically clear, the risks on both sides so great, and the imperative for choice so insistent as in our time. Political leaders in the countries that are making their appearance within the vast territories of the Soviet ex-empire must make up their minds more rapidly, more decisively, and with much greater awareness of the consequences of their decisions than was ever the case in the sleepwalking court of Louis XV. Moreover, their decisions will have repercussions beyond their own territories, as political leaders in Africa, Asia and Latin America also decide what to do in the face of current realities that are unbearable, and blueprints for change that appear unattainable.

What Walter Adams and James Brock have done is to present both sides of this debate in the form of a colloquy between a skeptical, wise, but extremely worried Prime Minister charged with making this fateful choice, and a hopeful, perhaps sometimes overly hopeful, Advisor who advocates a leap into capitalism. What the authors make clear is that this debate is not just an argument about economics, but about politics, and beyond politics, about the human propensities for risk-taking and for self-protection, for imagining the best and expecting the worst.

Adams and Brock manage to convey the feelings of both sides in this debate. On the whole their sympathies lie with the skeptical Prime Minister, but they are far from blind to the power of the arguments advanced by the Advisor. As a result the reader is constantly torn—now inclining to this side, now to the other—not least because the dialogue is both deadly serious, and laced with wit: one smiles and reaches for a pencil to underline such phrases as "Pessimism is informed optimism." It is educational in the best sense of the word, forcing us to experience the meaning of decisions that can so easily be presented as mere exercises in choice theory, not as the painful, risk-laden, never fully foreseeable bets that history forces the economist to make.

Robert Heilbroner

A Chronology of Revolution in Eastern Europe

1989–1992

March 27, 1989: Communist Party repudiated in free Soviet elections; Boris Yeltsin wins landslide election to Congress of Peoples Deputies.

April 20, 1989: Dissident Andrei Sakharov elected to Soviet Parliament.

June 4, 1989: Solidarity party wins decisive majority in free Polish elections.

July 23, 1989: Democratic Forum dominates free elections in Hungary.

September 23, 1989: Hungarian government orders removal of red star from all public buildings.

November 9, 1989: Berlin Wall dismantled.

November 22, 1989: Mass demonstrations trigger "Velvet Revolution" in Czechoslovakia.

November 24, 1989: Communist leadership resigns office in Czechoslovakia.

December 10, 1989: Polish authorities remove statue of Lenin in Nowa Huta.

December 17, 1989: Solidarity-led government announces radical program of economic reforms for Poland.

December 29, 1989: Dissident playwright Václav Havel elected president of Czechoslovakia.

January 1, 1990: "Big Bang" economic transformation program launched in Poland.

January 2, 1990: Demonstrations in Poland protest soaring prices and unemployment.

January 28, 1990: Polish Communist Party disbanded. McDonald's outlet opens in Moscow, dispensing "Bolshoi Maks."

January 30, 1990:   Mass demonstrations protest price inflation in Hungary and demand pay increases.

February 7, 1990:   Communist Party surrenders monopoly of political power in Soviet Union.

March 4, 1990:   Freely elected opposition parties win majority control in Moscow, Leningrad, and Kiev.

May 1, 1990:   Kremlin leaders jeered during May Day parade in Red Square.

June 21, 1990:   Budapest stock exchange opens.

September 17, 1990:   Hungarian privatization program begins.

October 2, 1990:   Unification of East and West Germany.

December 9, 1990:   Solidarity leader Lech Walesa elected president of Poland.

April 16, 1991:   Warsaw stock exchange opens.

June 28, 1991:   Communist trade bloc (Council for Mutual Economic Assistance [COMECON]) dissolved.

July 1, 1991:   Warsaw Pact dissolved.

October 27, 1991:   Soviet central planning agency (Gosplan) being phased out; thousands of economists reported to be looking for work.

December 8, 1991:   Leaders of Russia, Ukraine, and Byelorussia declare that the Soviet Union no longer exists and proclaim new "Commonwealth of Independent States."

January 5, 1992:   More than two hundred thousand East Germans estimated to have migrated west during past year, searching for work.

April 12, 1992:   Investment voucher privatization program begins in Czechoslovakia.

April 27, 1992: International Monetary Fund (IMF) and World Bank grant membership status to most former Soviet republics.

July 1992: Slovakia moves to form a sovereign state, independent from Czechoslovakia.

Adam Smith Goes to Moscow

*A Dialogue on
Radical Reform*

*The dialogue takes place
in a governmental palace
somewhere in Eastern
Europe, where an American
economist, invited for the
purpose, is advising
the leader of a newly
independent country.*

DAY 1 – THE AGENDA

---

*The path ahead is outlined. The conferees discuss
marketization, privatization, control of hyperinflation,
and the Big Bang model.*

PRIME MINISTER: First, let me welcome you to Eastern
Europe. We all appreciate your willingness to advise us
on the difficult task of transforming our command-
and-control economies into market economies.

ADVISOR: I am delighted to share with you the extensive
experience that Western economists, especially American experts, have accumulated over the years in dealing with these problems. You just can't believe the
pressure on us these days: I am personal advisor to
a number of other East European heads of state; the
U.S. Congress constantly invites me to testify on the
progress of economic transformation of communist
nations; requests for lectures, seminars, and media interviews never cease; publishers hound me for manu-
scripts and articles. It's a great relief to spend the week
with you, free from all the oppressive phone calls and
faxes.

PRIME MINISTER: You are familiar with what we in Eastern Europe have been through in the last seventy-five
years. In the former Soviet Union under Lenin and Stalin, we were subjected to revolution, civil war, mass
expropriation of property, and mass collectivization of
farming, as well as mass famine and mass murder.
After World War II, during the Khrushchev and Brezh-

nev years, the dictatorship was softened somewhat. Gorbachev gave us *glasnost* and the glimmerings of personal freedom, but his halfhearted gestures to *perestroika*—what you call "restructuring"—brought us the economic gloom of hyperinflation. Forty years of Communist rule in Hungary, Poland, Czechoslovakia, and the other Soviet satellites produced similar devastation—an unproductive economy, a fundamentally distorted price system, and nagging shortages of consumer goods. Like the former Soviet Union, these countries paid a heavy price for the Cold War in terms of resources diverted from the civilian to the military economy—something they could ill afford.

ADVISOR: History has not been kind to the countries in this region.

PRIME MINISTER: And now we are embarked on an experiment that has never been attempted before. In the West—and this is something your economists tend to forget—the market system did not spring forth full-blown and overnight. It was not the product of radical, deliberate social engineering. Instead, it was the end result of a millennium of slow, almost imperceptible evolutionary change.[1]

By contrast, all our countries have to some extent inherited the antidemocratic traditions of tsarist Russia—centuries of a patriarchal, authoritarian culture. Even Stalin's personality cult was not just imposed from above; it also grew from below. We're trying to overcome these traditions, but they aren't dead yet.

---

[1] Robert Heilbroner, *The Making of Economic Society*, 8th ed. (Englewood Cliffs, N.J.: Prentice Hall, 1989).

And you know the old saying: The dead always seize the living by the throat.[2]

Now we're not only trying to embrace democratic institutions, but to create a market economy at one and the same time—with a single stroke. It is a unique moment in history, and neither past experience nor current economic doctrine provides helpful guidance for the task before us.

ADVISOR: It is always tempting to regard one's problems as unique. This is a mistake. After many years of research on a good number of countries desirous of reform, I have come to the following conclusion: The circumstances of these countries were not entirely the same, and each regarded its own situation as special. But certain common elements existed. For example, the principles of physics apply in all nations; by the same token, the basic principles of economics are applicable in all nations. The most essential of these principles is the relationship between economic prosperity and private property rights.[3]

PRIME MINISTER: You seem to be saying that the same boilerplate advice is relevant to all nations, irrespective of their history, culture, traditions, or stage of development—that there are iron laws of economics, which are universal and eternal. I don't believe that. I am convinced that we must learn from the experience of other nations—that we must, for example, carefully and at-

[2] Stephen F. Cohen and Katrina Vanden Heuvel, *Voices of Glasnost: Interviews with Gorbachev's Reformers* (New York: W. W. Norton, 1989), 187, 196.

[3] Milton Friedman, *Friedman in China* (Hong Kong: Chinese University Press, 1990). See also Stanley Fischer, "Eastern Europe's Transition," *Challenge*, Sept.–Oct. 1990, 6.

tentively study the recommendations of the International Monetary Fund (IMF). But I am also convinced that in order to grow an apple tree in a place with a different climate, you must choose the right kind of tree and not try, as some have already done, to grow apples at the North Pole.[4]

ADVISOR: Let me draw on our experience in Latin America. Forget geography for a moment and put Poland in the place of Argentina, Hungary in the place of Uruguay. You will see states that are weak as organizations; political parties and other associations that are ineffectual in representing and mobilizing the people; economies that are monopolistic, overprotected, and overregulated; agricultures that are poorly designed to feed the people; public bureaucracies that are overgrown; welfare services that are fragmentary and rudimentary. And will you not conclude that such conditions breed governments vulnerable to pressure from large firms, populist movements of doubtful commitment to democratic institutions, armed forces that sit menacingly on the sidelines, church hierarchies torn between authoritarianism and social justice, and nationalist sentiments vulnerable to xenophobia?[5]

PRIME MINISTER: Nevertheless, it seems to me that we can't ignore local circumstances that influence people's receptivity to new ideas and to revolutionary change. Consider, for example, that in 1990, according to Moscow's Center of Public Opinion Studies, 42 percent of the Soviet people believed in telepathy, 57 per-

---

[4] Alexander N. Yakovlev, "Twilight in Russia," *NPQ*, Fall 1992, 55.
[5] Adam Przeworski, *Democracy and the Market* (New York: Cambridge University Press, 1991), 191.

cent believed in televised cures for afflictions of all sorts, 42 percent believed in astrology, and 35 percent believed in sorcery. The pollsters found a widespread belief in UFOs, parapsychology, and mystic medicine, along with deeply ingrained racial, religious, and ethnic prejudice. In the last Czech election, forty parties, coalitions and movements contended for votes, including the "Friends of Beer" and the "Independent Erotic Initiative." Obviously, this bizarre milieu is a fertile habitat for economic myths and a suspicion of free market ideas imported from the alien West.

ADVISOR: That's true. As Oscar Wilde once said, people will believe anything provided it's sufficiently incredible. But once a market economy takes hold, a rational belief system and rational behavior will dissipate— and, eventually, eliminate—prevailing myth and superstition.

PRIME MINISTER: You realize, of course, that our transition to a market economy is not taking place in a vacuum. We confront military crises all over the map: a shooting war among the republics of what was once the Yugoslav confederation; a dispute between Russia and the Ukraine over control of the Black Sea fleet; a wrangle among the member states of the former Soviet Union over the ownership of nuclear weapons and the responsibility for their scheduled destruction. We confront crises arising from ethnic and nationalist strife: the clamor of Slovak nationalists to secede from the Czechoslovak Republic; the desire of the Hungarian minority in Romania to be reunited with their original homeland; the sentiment in Moldavia for annexation by Romania. We confront constitutional crises: the Russian problem, for example, in creating the kind of legal infrastructure in which private property is legitimized and in which a market economy can flourish.

ADVISOR: You have to face up to these crises systematically and methodically.

PRIME MINISTER: Suppose we can surmount these non-economic problems. How does a free market come into being? Is it a gift of nature? Does it spring full-blown, as Athena from Zeus's brow?

ADVISOR: Markets will arise naturally to integrate and co-ordinate economic activity.[6] Professor Friedman, whom you have met on a number of occasions, has illustrated the process with an interesting example. "How did language develop?" he asks. "In much the same way as an economic order develops through the market—out of the voluntary interaction of individuals, in this case seeking to trade ideas or information or gossip rather than goods and services with one another. One or another meaning was attributed to a word, or words were added as the need arose. Grammatical usages developed and were later codified into rules. Two parties who want to communicate with one another both benefit from coming to a common agreement about the words they use. As a wider and wider circle of people find it advantageous to communicate with one another, a common usage spreads and is codified in dictionaries. At no point is there any coercion, any central planner who has power to command, though in more recent times government school systems have placed an important role in standardizing usage."[7]

---

[6] János Kornai, *The Road to a Free Economy* (New York: W. W. Norton, 1990), 36.

[7] Milton Friedman and Rose Friedman, *Free to Choose* (New York: Harcourt, Brace Jovanovich, 1980), 17.

PRIME MINISTER: That's an interesting excursion into linguistic anthropology. But what's the moral of the story? Are you telling me that the free market will develop naturally—that it will naturally overcome the oppressive legacy of history, culture, politics, nationalism, and traditional institutions?

ADVISOR: In time, yes.

PRIME MINISTER: But time is a precious commodity. The ice is thin, and we have a long way to go. After decades of communist rule, few people have any idea of what private property means or how markets function. Everybody supports "privatization" of state industries, for example, but nobody seems to know how to go about it, or even how to sort out what belongs to which public authority. Everybody is for a "market economy"; but the lifting of price controls has had little effect, except to raise prices to astronomical levels. Our people are impatient with abstract theories concocted by Western economists for recitation by an intellectual elite in countries targeted for reform.

ADVISOR: Costs inevitably accompany the transition from a command-and-control system to a free economy. The people will come to appreciate their new freedom soon enough.

PRIME MINISTER: What are the most important components of a market transition plan?

ADVISOR: The reform plan of the IMF, which, incidentally, has been tested in many countries around the world, prescribes the essential steps you must take.[8]

---

[8] *The Economy of the USSR: Summary and Recommendations* (Washington, D.C.: International Monetary Fund, International Bank for Reconstruction and Development, Organization for Economic Cooperation and

PRIME MINISTER: Sometimes the IMF experts remind me of those medieval doctors who—no matter what the ailment—prescribed the same remedy: apply leeches and bleed the patient.

ADVISOR: Well, be that as it may, according to the IMF, the first component of the transition is marketization. In the Russian case, for example, you must abolish the government's thoroughgoing, centralized control of the economy. You must eliminate state planning, which tries to balance more than fifty thousand inputs, raw materials, and intermediate goods—a task requiring the handling of some seven million documents annually, and some eighty-three million calculations, half of which subsequently have to be changed. You must abolish the intricately detailed production orders issued by central planners to enterprise managers: Gosplan, the highest planning commission, issuing two thousand sets of production instructions for such major product groups as "construction materials"; Gossnab, the state material supply commission, dividing these into fifteen thousand narrower categories,

---

Development, and European Bank for Reconstruction and Development, 1990). The foremost exponent of this strategy for Eastern Europe—the so-called Big Bang approach—is Professor Jeffrey Sachs of Harvard. David Lipton and Jeffrey Sachs, "Creating a Market Economy in Eastern Europe: The Case of Poland," *Brookings Papers on Economic Activity* 1 (1990): 100; id., "Privatization in Eastern Europe: The Case of Poland," in Vittorio Corbo, Fabrizio Coricelli and Jan Bossak, eds., *Reforming Central and Eastern European Economics* (Washington, D. C.: World Bank, 1991), 293–334. In the same vein, see Merton J. Peck and Thomas J. Richardson, eds., *What Is to Be Done? Proposals for the Soviet Transition to the Market* (New Haven: Yale University Press, 1991), and Olivier Blanchard, Rudiger Dornbusch, Paul Krugman, Richard Layard, and Lawrence Summers, *Reform in Eastern Europe* (Cambridge, Mass.: MIT Press, 1991), xiii. For proposals to implement the Big Bang strategy in China, see *Friedman in China.*

such as "lumber"; various subministries further dividing them into fifty thousand more detailed product segments (shingles, beams, boards), and into literally millions of specific products (large, medium, and small shingles)![9]

You must abandon the absolutely bizarre centrally planned quota system, which results in perfectly good zinc's being turned into scrap metal in order to fulfill the plan for nonferrous metal waste; perfectly good tractors, being driven miles for unneeded repairs in order to meet the annual quota for tractor repairs; and the literal tearing apart of truck chassis by bus factories because it is easier to smash off unwanted parts with sledgehammers than it is to alter physical production orders issued by central planning agencies.[10]

You must eliminate the State Price Committee, which sets about two hundred thousand prices per year—some at such perversely ridiculous levels that peasants feed their livestock with bread purchased from shop shelves at 1955 prices[11] and upwards of a quarter of your industries produce *negative* value added, that is, manufacture goods whose output value is less than the cost of the inputs used to produce them.[12] In short, you must reject the principles of so-

[9] Robert L. Heilbroner, "Reflections after Communism," *New Yorker,* Sept. 10, 1990, 93; Alec Nove, *The Soviet Economic System,* 3d ed. (London: Unwin Hyman, 1986), 19; Robert C. Stuart and Paul R. Gregory, *Soviet Economic Structure and Performance,* 4th ed. (New York: Harper and Row, 1990).

[10] Nikolai Shmelev and Vladimir Popov, *The Turning Point: Revitalizing the Soviet Economy* (New York: Doubleday, 1989), 113, 121.

[11] Marshall I. Goldman, *Gorbachev's Challenge* (New York: W. W. Norton, 1987), 28, 35.

[12] OECD, *Reforming the Economies of Central and Eastern Europe* (Paris: OECD, 1992), 19; "Russia's Value Gap," *Economist,* Oct. 24, 1992, 75.

cialist planning, which many of your own experts now characterize as the economics of the lunatic asylum. You must allow the free market to set prices and to correct the pervasive distortions which plague your economy. Decentralized, unimpeded decisionmaking must be allowed to produce spontaneous economic order.

PRIME MINISTER: Spontaneous order, or spontaneous combustion? I needn't tell you that the immediate effect of such a policy would be a precipitous increase in prices and rampant inflation. If wages are not allowed to rise proportionately, that would mean a sharp drop in our people's standard of living. How can we explain that to a senior citizen whose monthly pension is suddenly just enough to buy a few pounds of sausage? [*Gesturing toward an easel*] As you can see from the comparative statistics in Chart 1, we have a razor-thin margin of error. When people are hungry, they won't settle for a diet of lofty ideals.

ADVISOR: People don't want realism; they want magic. But they have to realize that, in a market economy, they would still be better off than they were under the old regime. If goods have a low official price but you cannot buy them, then in effect you don't have low-priced goods. If you spend five hours in a queue to purchase something, that price is not low either—at least not if you value your time as well as your money. My neighbor recently told me an old story: There are two butcher shops on opposite sides of a street, one facing the other. A customer goes to one of them to buy mutton and complains about the high price. The shopkeeper replies, "If you think our mutton is expensive, go across the street—it is cheap there. But there is no

CHART 1. ECONOMIC INDICATORS AND INFANT MORTALITY
RATES IN SELECTED EAST EUROPEAN COUNTRIES AND THE
UNITED STATES, 1988

	GDP (billions of dollars)	Per Capita GDP (dollars)	Number of People per:		Infant Mortality Rate (per 1,000 births)
			Car	TV	
Czechoslovakia	43	2,737	5.7	3.0	12
Hungary	28	2,625	6.4	13.0	17
Poland	65	1,719	9.0	4.4	16
Romania	32	1,374	81.1	4.0	22
Soviet Union	583	2,055	22.8	9.4	25
Yugoslavia	54	2,279	7.8	2.2	25
United States	4,881	19,815	1.8	1.2	10

Source: Adapted from Book of Vital World Statistics (New York: Times Books, 1990).
Note: Amounts are in 1988 dollars.

mutton in the other shop!" So what is the use of low prices? Realistically, your old system of controls did not give you low prices, but high prices.[13]

PRIME MINISTER: So marketization, the first major component of the transition, means getting rid of the central planning. What's the second major component?

ADVISOR: Comprehensive privatization.[14] This is absolutely crucial. The government must get out of the business of running business. Your central planners do not—and cannot—know what the microrequirements of the economy are. They do not—and cannot—determine the most economical way of achieving their

[13] Friedman in China, 1990.
[14] Jeffrey D. Sachs, "Privatization in Russia: Some Lessons from Eastern Europe," American Economic Review 82 (May 1992):43–48.

overall production objectives. No conceivable set of incentives and success indicators can be laid down by the center to ensure that enterprise management will efficiently meet the disaggregated needs of industry and society. The multiplicity of plan targets inevitably—and unavoidably—suffers from inconsistencies and contradictions; compulsory production quotas and tightly administered supply-rationing systems frustrate initiative at the enterprise level; and bureaucratic evaluation of plan fulfillment rewards those who aim low, while encouraging hoarding of materials and over-applications for material inputs.[15]

PRIME MINISTER: Your critique reminds me of a World War II experience: Our long-range weather forecasts were shown to be statistically worthless; the forecasters themselves requested that they be discontinued. Their petition was denied with the following reply: "The Commanding General is well aware that the forecasts are no good. However, he needs them for planning purposes."[16]

ADVISOR: In the economic sphere, the consequences of state ownership are abysmal. As one result, your investment construction periods are four times longer than those in the West, which causes "unfinished" projects to soar, and plants to be obsolete long before they're completed. As another result, your inventory ratios are double, triple, and even quadruple those in Western industry, while your gross domestic material output per worker is 40–50 percent below U.S. levels.[17]

---

[15] Nove, *Soviet Economic System*, 161–62, 388–89, 394–95.

[16] Kenneth J. Arrow, "I Know a Hawk from a Handsaw," in Michael Szenberg, ed., *Eminent Economists* (Cambridge: Cambridge University Press, 1992), 46–47.

[17] Nove, *Soviet Economic System*, 109, 154–57; Abram Bergson, *Plan-*

That is why state property—from the giant state monopolies down to the state-operated retail stores—must be transferred to private citizens. That's the only way to inject efficiency, entrepreneurship, and rationality into a comatose economy.

PRIME MINISTER: You know, of course, that sizable segments of our population—especially conservatives and hard-line communists—have serious objections to mass privatization. Some say that it will undermine the authority of the state. Others say it will permit crooks, mafias, and the *nomenklatura* (the old management bureaucracy) to seize the country's wealth. Yet others fear that it will allow foreigners to buy up the country's assets, effectively turning its citizens into economic slaves.

ADVISOR: Those are spurious arguments, and you must not let them deter you from doing what needs to be done.

PRIME MINISTER: Well, I don't think the people's fears of nomenklatura privatization and/or foreign control are unfounded, but I do see the overriding need for the privatization as well as the marketization. And what's the third component of the transition?

ADVISOR: You must adopt a stringent fiscal and monetary policy to avert the dangers of hyperinflation.[18] This means drastic action to eliminate the budget deficits, which currently account for anywhere from 5 to 20 percent of GDP in the region. It means an end to the huge increase in the national debt . . .

---

ning and Performance in Socialist Economies (London: Unwin Hyman, 1989), 35.

[18] Peck and Richardson, *What Is to Be Done?* 29–33.

PRIME MINISTER: Forgive me for interrupting. If we agree to balance the budget in economies that have produced virtually no wealth in years, half of our people will starve. Besides, the United States is hardly a good role model of fiscal responsibility. Isn't it true that, over the last dozen years, you have increased your national debt from one trillion to four trillion dollars? That over this period the United States has been transformed from the largest creditor nation to the largest debtor nation in the world? That you seem congenitally incapable of controlling your annual budget deficit, which is currently estimated to exceed four hundred billion dollars? Why do you expect our government to accomplish what yours has apparently found to be impossible?

ADVISOR: That's true, but you are not as rich as the United States. Therefore, you don't have the luxury of imitating its fiscal mismanagement. You have to impose tight fiscal restraints if you want to avoid hyperinflation. And you must supplement them with a tough monetary policy. You have to stop printing money recklessly. You have to shut off the faucet of credit. The banks have to stop extending loans to the inefficient state enterprises—loans that neither the lender nor the borrowers expect will ever have to be repaid. In short, fiscal and monetary discipline are indispensable components of a successful transition policy.

PRIME MINISTER: That sounds like a lecture straight out of an economics text. I agree that in principle budgetary and monetary austerity should be the order of the day. But we don't live in a textbook world. We have to be pragmatic. How can we suddenly cut off all subsidies and essential credit to the giant state-owned en-

CHART 2. UNEMPLOYMENT ESTIMATES FOR SELECTED
EAST EUROPEAN COUNTRIES, 1992–1994 (PERCENT OF
WORKFORCE)

	1992	1993	1994
Czecholosvakia	8.0	13.0	17.0
Hungary	14.0	18.6	19.9
Poland	15.0	19.0	19.8
Romania	10.6	13.6	16.5
Former Soviet Union	0.2	15.0	24.4

Source: Adapted from Tim Carrington, "Eastern Europe's Ills May Defy Usual Cures," Wall Street Journal, Dec. 7, 1992, 1.

terprises that account for the lion's share of industrial production? How can we—overnight—shut down the redundant military-industrial complex? If we do, these enterprises are doomed to bankruptcy and the millions of workers they employ are condemned to unemployment. [Flipping to another chart] As you can see on Chart 2, in a forecast prepared by your own Morgan Stanley investment bank, the outlook under the best of circumstances seems dismal. As it is our national income has already plunged by a third—a collapse equivalent to that of the U.S. economy during the Depression.[19] To trigger further decline would be the making of both an economic and a political catastrophe.

ADVISOR: You just have to make up your mind to bite the bullet. As the great nineteenth-century Hungarian reform politician István Széchenyi put it, the dentist is cruel to pull slowly and faintly on a diseased tooth over

[19] Grigorii Khanin, "The Soviet Economy—From Crisis to Collapse," in Anders Aslund, ed., The Post-Soviet Economy: Soviet and Western Perspectives (New York: St. Martin's Press, 1992) 16.

a period of days. To shrink from what needs to be done merely prolongs the pain and agony.[20]

PRIME MINISTER: What role remains for government in a market economy?

ADVISOR: Government has a vital role to play, but one that must be narrowly circumscribed: Government must establish the legal foundation for the market system—the rules of the game—and serve as referee in enforcing those rules. It must define private property, adjudicate disputes, and establish a system of commercial law. Having done this, government must then refrain from interfering. For you, the task is to drastically shrink the size and influence of the state.

PRIME MINISTER: Suppose we had the necessary infrastructure—which, of course, we don't. On which front should we move first? What is the appropriate sequence of steps to take?

ADVISOR: One of the essential characteristics of a market economy is its interdependence. What happens in one sector feeds back to other sectors. The priorities for action I have just outlined must be implemented simultaneously and, in view of your growing economic crisis, immediately. They must be implemented with a "Big Bang" to produce the desired results. Each of my major recommendations reinforces the others. If adopted together, they can be successful. If adopted incrementally, over a long period of time, they are almost certain to fail.[21]

PRIME MINISTER: That's a tall order. Isn't there a danger,

---

[20] Quoted in Kornai, *Road to a Free Economy,* 161.

[21] Lipton and Sachs, "Creating a Market Economy," 99–100; Peck and Richardson, *What Is to Be Done?* 9, 21.

as the Russians say, that if you chase after two rabbits, you won't catch even one. As it is, we sometimes feel as if we were driving a car at dizzying speed down a superhighway and at the same time trying to repair the transmission, change the tires, and in some instances even replace the engine.

ADVISOR: Yet the attempt has to be made if your goal is an efficiently functioning market economy.

PRIME MINISTER: Back in the 1960s and 1970s, we thought that once we ditched our ideological baggage, the switch to a market-based economy would be easy. In the last five years, we have become not only older but wiser. The fact is that not a single socialist economy in Eastern Europe has yet been able to effectuate anything like a satisfactory transition. Indeed, given the pain of the transition to a market economy, many of our people now long for the security and predictability of life under the old order. I'm sure you have heard the ghoulish joke currently circulating in Moscow. Question: "What has one year of capitalism achieved that seventy-five years of communism could not?" Answer: "To make communism look good."[22]

ADVISOR: That's because all your attempts to reform up to now have been piecemeal and halfhearted. I remind you of Lenin's dictum that progress requires two steps forward and one step back. Gradual reform may amount to the reverse: one step forward and two steps back. The gradual approach may thwart reform altogether.[23]

[22] Quoted in Thomas E. Weisskopf, "Russia in Transition," *Challenge* (Nov.–Dec. 1992): 37.

[23] Lipton and Sachs, "Creating a Market Economy," 99–100; Anne O. Krueger, "Institutions for the New Private Sector," in Christopher Clague and

PRIME MINISTER: Communism, it used to be said, was a fine creed in theory but too pure for human beings. If we go ahead with the Big Bang, we may prove that the same is true of free market economics. A sudden lurch to laissez-faire may well cause pain that is too great and popular resistance that is too strong. It may produce "shock" but without "therapy."

ADVISOR: What are the alternatives? Suppose the British were to decide to switch from driving on the left side of the road to the right side? Would you recommend that they do so gradually, starting with trucks one year and cars a year later?[24]

PRIME MINISTER: Good point! You've had a long day. May I suggest that we reconvene tomorrow and begin to discuss your reform agenda one item at a time.

ADVISOR: That's fine with me. Just promise that you'll disconnect my telephone!

Gordon C. Rausser, eds., *The Emergence of Market Economies in Eastern Europe* (Cambridge, Mass.: Blackwell, 1992), 223.

[24] Jeffrey Sachs, "The Economic Transformation of Eastern Europe: The Case of Poland," *The American Economist* 36 (Fall 1992): 5.

Day 2 — Marketization

Immediate and total price decontrol is recommended. The conferees discuss the invisible hand, income differentials, soft budget constraints, and temporary hyperinflation as an unavoidable trade-off.

PRIME MINISTER: It's obvious that our centrally controlled command economy has failed. But I don't see how we can rely on uncoordinated, voluntary individual choice to perform in any better fashion. For example, if we want to produce wheat, don't we also have to ensure the production of a sufficient number of tractors to harvest the wheat crop?

ADVISOR: Of course.

PRIME MINISTER: Don't we also have to arrange to produce a sufficient amount of steel in order to manufacture the tractors needed to harvest the wheat crop?

ADVISOR: Certainly.

PRIME MINISTER: Don't we also have to undertake to refine enough gasoline to operate the tractors?

ADVISOR: Indeed.

PRIME MINISTER: And isn't the same true of tires, glass, drive shafts, fan belts and myriad other tractor parts, not to mention crude oil for refining into fuel, and iron ore for producing steel?

ADVISOR: Yes.

PRIME MINISTER: Now, as commissar of economic planning, I can directly coordinate the production of all these materials in just the right amounts needed to ensure that the wheat crop can be harvested.

ADVISOR: Your deplorable agricultural record suggests otherwise. The former Soviet republics—once the world's largest grain exporters—have under the Stalinist model become the world's largest grain importers; despite vast grazing lands, they are among the world's largest meat importers; a quarter to possibly as much as one-half of their crops rot in the fields; and half of their milk production spoils because of insufficient refrigeration. Meanwhile, private peasant plots, representing a mere 3 percent of their arable lands, produce approximately one-quarter of their entire annual crop output, including 30 percent of their meat and milk, over 40 percent of their fruits, berries, and eggs, and 60 percent of their potatoes.[1]

PRIME MINISTER: That may be. Still, if all these decisions are left to voluntary individual choice, how can I possibly be sure that the right amount of all these articles will be forthcoming? Granted, our central planning performance has been less than spectacular. But the chance of uncoordinated, independent producers doing any better—the probability that independent producers would all somehow miraculously make precisely the right decisions—seems to me to be much smaller.

ADVISOR: It seems improbable because you haven't grasped the fundamental principles according to which markets coordinate the decisions of free individuals—the process Adam Smith called the invisible hand.

PRIME MINISTER: It sounds metaphysical to me.

---

[1] Marshall I. Goldman, *USSR in Crisis: The Failure of an Economic System* (New York: W. W. Norton, 1983), 2; and id., *Gorbachev's Challenge* (New York: W. W. Norton, 1987), 33–37.

ADVISOR: Regardless of how it may sound to you, it is essential to the functioning of the free market. The heart of the market system's capacity to coordinate individual decisionmaking is the profit motive, acting through the forces of supply and demand. In your wheat example, the farmers in a free market presumably choose to grow wheat because it is profitable for them to produce it.

PRIME MINISTER: That seems a reasonable assumption.

ADVISOR: And in order to produce wheat, the farmers will need to purchase tractors in order to harvest their wheat. This demand by farmers for tractors will make the production of tractors profitable, and will attract others into the business of tractor manufacturing—not to help farmers, but because they can earn more income supplying the tractors for which farmers are willing to pay. Tractor producers, in turn, will want to buy steel and other parts. This, too, will attract people into producing them—again, not because of an altruistic desire to aid tractor manufacturers, but because there is income to be made in supplying them. It is through this interaction of demand and supply—driven by the profit motive—that the free market coordinates the decisions of all these independent producers.

PRIME MINISTER: It all seems to hinge on the basest of human motives—greed and selfishness. As the Russian proverb has it, he who is greedy won't even share ice with you in the winter.

ADVISOR: It's not greed, but the desire to better one's lot. It is one of the most powerful, durable, and dependable of human motives. As Adam Smith put it in his great economic manifesto, *The Wealth of Nations*, "It is not from the benevolence of the butcher, the brewer, or the baker, that we expect our dinner, but from their regard to their own interest. We address ourselves, not to their humanity but to their self-love, and never talk to them of our own necessities but of their advantages" (p. 14).[2] It was Adam Smith who demonstrated compellingly how the alchemy of the market system transforms crass self-interest into social service. The secret of its success is simple: it lets you do well by doing good.

PRIME MINISTER: It seems simple, perhaps too simple. Suppose the tractor manufacturers were to produce more tractors than farmers wish to buy. Surely, you can't deny that this is a plausible possibility?

ADVISOR: Not at all. But we can depend on free market forces of supply and demand to correct the problem. Once the tractor manufacturers discover that they have produced too many tractors, and that this is unprofitable, they will do two things. First, they will lower their prices in order to sell their inventory of unsold tractors. Second, they will reduce their planned rate of tractor production in order to avoid such excess output in the future. Through these adjustments in price and quantity, the tractor market will return to equilibrium: the quantity of tractors produced will decline into balance with the quantity of tractors farmers wish to buy.

PRIME MINISTER: And if, instead, too few tractors are produced?

ADVISOR: The same process will work in reverse. The excess demand for tractors by farmers will cause the price of tractors to rise, create abnormally high profits in

---

[2] All the Adam Smith quotes are from Adam Smith, *The Wealth of Nations*, 5th (last) ed. (1789; reprint, New York: Modern Library, 1937).

tractor manufacturing, and thereby induce existing tractor producers to expand their output volume in order to capture these excess profits. High profits will also lure new producers into the tractor business, further expanding tractor production, until tractor output rises to match the farmers' demand. Once again, in the long run, just the right number of tractors will be produced.

PRIME MINISTER: And the same would apply to product markets up and down the line, from gasoline and tire production, to tractor parts and components?

ADVISOR: Absolutely.

PRIME MINISTER: Without the need for any direct coordination by a centralized government planning agency?

ADVISOR: As Adam Smith said, as if by an invisible hand.

PRIME MINISTER: But suppose an industry other than tractors—home refrigerators, say—unexpectedly buys steel intended for tractor production. Now there won't be enough tractors to harvest the wheat crop. Now your invisible hand will have dealt us a fine slap.

ADVISOR: Not at all. What you have described is an increase in the demand for steel. Again, the free market will adjust to this development in a predictable and desirable way: In the short run, the excess demand will trigger a rise in steel prices, in order to allocate now-scarce steel supplies among buyers who value them the most, who can put them to the most profitable use, and hence who are willing to pay the highest price for them.

PRIME MINISTER: This is madness! What can be more valuable than food? How can you say such a thing?

ADVISOR: I'm not saying it; the market is.

PRIME MINISTER: Your free market is a wondrous thing! It even speaks.

ADVISOR: Quite articulately, as a matter of fact. In a free market system, it is consumers, not you or I, who are sovereign. The reason refrigerator manufacturers are increasing their production, and buying more steel, can only be that consumers have decided they wish to buy more refrigerators, thereby rendering increased refrigerator production more profitable than before. Your personal values are irrelevant, as are mine. The market speaks on behalf of consumers and their aggregate desires, as expressed by their collective willingness to pay.

PRIME MINISTER: But what will the fools put in their refrigerators, if there aren't enough tractors available to harvest the crops?

ADVISOR: They'll put food in them, and if you'll permit me to proceed I'll demonstrate how. Understanding the working of the free market requires that you follow a complete sequence of steps of economic cause and effect. As I said, the short-run effect will be an increase in the price of steel. But the market adjustment process doesn't stop there. Higher steel prices render steel production more profitable than before. Induced by these higher profits, existing steel producers will increase their steel production and expand their operations. New producers will also be enticed by high profits to enter the steel business, to construct new facilities, and further to expand the overall volume of steel production. Expansion of output and increased competition will also act to push steel prices down. This long-run adjustment will take time, but in the end there will be more steel available to produce more refrigerators and more tractors. In other words, there will be both refrigerators *and* food to put in them—consumers will be able to have their cakes and refrigerate them too.

PRIME MINISTER: What you are describing is the apportionment of a nation's resources—its workforce, land, factories, raw materials—among the production of food, tractors, and refrigerators.

ADVISOR: You are exactly right. In precise economic terminology, this is how the market system allocates and constantly reallocates a society's scarce resources among alternative uses, without the need for centralized government direction and control.

PRIME MINISTER: This reminds me of an old joke: How many laissez-faire economists does it take to change a light bulb? None. They sit in the dark and wait for the invisible hand to do it. Surely you must admit that some needs take priority over others—that food production must take priority over the manufacture of hula hoops. In the early days of perestroika, for example, Russian hospitals were suddenly unable to obtain hypodermic needles, because the directors of the enterprise that produced the syringes switched to the production of more profitable items.[3] What ensures that the market system will first allocate our national resources to the most important uses, before allocating the remainder to more frivolous fields?

ADVISOR: Again, it is neither your priorities nor mine that matter. It is not for you or me to determine what is frivolous and what is not. It is the aggregate priorities

[3] Joseph S. Berliner, "Restructuring the Soviet Planned Economy," in William S. Kern, ed., *From Socialism to Market Economy* (Kalamazoo, Mich.: Upjohn Institute, 1992), 65.

of your nation's consumers, considered collectively, that determine national economic priorities. The things consumers desire the most will attract the greatest demand and hence will exhibit the highest relative profitability. The profit motive ensures that producers and resources will first be drawn to these fields. They will continue to enter and to expand these fields until prices and profitability decline. At this point, other, relatively more profitable fields will rise in priority and begin to attract resources. In the end, the equality of relative profits across markets and industries will ensure that all economically viable needs will have been met, and in the right mix, too. In technical terms, allocative efficiency will have been achieved.

PRIME MINISTER: Of course, you are ignoring the crucial role in this allocation process played by the distribution of income among consumers. After all, isn't it the amount of his or her income that determines whether or not an individual consumer's preferences count? If I have no income, won't my preferences and desires be ignored by your market system? More generally, wouldn't the market system's ranking of priorities reflect the distribution of income among the people? And if that distribution of income were altered, wouldn't your market system generate a different list of priorities, and yield a different mix of goods and services?

ADVISOR: Of course it would. But you have to understand that prices play a key role in determining the distribution of income. In fact, prices create incentives for the beneficial outcomes I have described precisely because they determine who gets what and how much. As Professor Friedman points out, if one's income depends on what one does—if it depends on the difference between the prices one receives for selling one's services and the prices one pays for the items one buys—then individuals have a strong incentive to ensure that they sell their services in the best market for the highest price, produce goods at the least cost, and produce those goods for which others are willing to pay the most.

PRIME MINISTER: My Polish friends say that whoever wishes to be rich must become a pig. But if I understand your argument, the income received by a person in a market system reflects his or her economic usefulness.

ADVISOR: Quite so. A market economy is a performance economy, in which monetary reward is obtained for personal productivity and contribution to the aggregate social product. If a person provides services that the society values highly—if he or she is economically valuable to the society—then the market reward in terms of income received will be relatively great. This is the justice of the market. High incomes are high because they reflect high contribution to output. Conversely, people with relatively low physical productivity compete by receiving still lower money wages.[4] Your grin suggests that you find this unexpectedly amusing.

PRIME MINISTER: I apologize. Your theory is so logical in the abstract. But the real world seems to refute it.

ADVISOR: In what way?

PRIME MINISTER: One example is the recent scandal of executive compensation paid by some of your large

[4] William R. Allen, *The Midnight Economist* (San Francisco: Institute for Contemporary Studies, 1989), 10, 95.

U.S. corporations—firms whose deplorable profit-and-loss statements contradict your productivity/performance justification for income differentials. Take the Big Three auto moguls, for example, who accompanied then-President George Bush on his 1992 trip to Tokyo. Despite the fact that they had presided over losses in sales, losses in market share, losses in jobs, and multibillion-dollar losses for their companies, they were paid vastly greater incomes than those of their far more successful Japanese counterparts. Chrysler chairman Lee Iacocca's 1991 compensation of $4.65 million was approximately ten times the amount paid Honda's highly successful chief executive officer, an astonishing pattern that is not atypical in U.S. industry. Even your own *Wall Street Journal*, hardly a bastion of bolshevism, has decried this as an embarrassment to free market advocates.[5] It certainly appears to turn your market reward system upside down.

ADVISOR: Unlike economics, management compensation is not an exact science.

PRIME MINISTER: It strikes many as outrageously unfair.

ADVISOR: Life is not fair! Unfairness takes many forms. Consider the inheritance of talent—musical ability, strength, mathematical genius. There is nothing fair about Madonna's having been endowed with a captivating voice, or Muhammad Ali's having been born with the skill of a great boxer. What kind of world

[5] The data on executive compensation are from Graef S. Crystal, *In Search of Excess: The Overcompensation of American Executives* (New York: W.W. Norton, 1991). The *Wall Street Journal*'s comment appeared in Paul A. Gigot, "Executive Pay—An Embarrassment to Free Marketers," *Wall Street Journal*, Jan. 10, 1992, A8.

would it be if everyone were a duplicate of everyone else?[6]

PRIME MINISTER: I suppose managerial incompetence may also be inherited, although I fail to comprehend why your market system should reward it so lavishly. But let's return to the role of prices in a market system: With everyone making economic decisions concerning production, profits, and the allocation of resources, the total amount of information required for the system to function must be overwhelming. In our command economy, only the central planners require this kind of detailed economic data. In the market system, however, every businessperson would seem to require massive computer banks of information. A crushing waste of duplicated calculation seems unavoidable.

ADVISOR: To the contrary, the beauty of the free market system is that it economizes on information, and efficiently directs information only to those who have a need to know.

PRIME MINISTER: In what way?

ADVISOR: Through prices, the central nervous system of a free market economy. Prices of outputs and inputs compactly provide all the information necessary. In our steel example, steel producers don't need to know whether the demand for steel has increased because of expanded refrigerator production or whether it is due to an increase in the popularity of weightlifting and bodybuilding. They don't even have to know that something called the "demand" for steel exists and that it has increased. All they need to know is that

---

[6] Milton Friedman and Rose Friedman, *Free to Choose* (New York: Harcourt, Brace Jovanovich, 1980), 127–28.

buyers are willing to pay more for steel; these higher prices will make it worthwhile for them to expand their production of steel. Moreover, only those interested in steel—producing it or buying it—will respond to the signals sent by steel prices. Others will ignore them, since they are unaffected. Only those who need the information will obtain it.

PRIME MINISTER: But how can you be sure that producers will be attentive to the information conveyed by prices, and that they will act upon it expeditiously? As an economic planner, I can assure you that my experience has been that people ignore my memorandums and orders unless I constantly badger them—telephone them, issue follow-up requests, visit and revisit them. It consumes my life and is eternally frustrating.

ADVISOR: The beauty of the market system is that profits and losses provide the most persuasive incentive for people to respond with alacrity to price signals. Those who don't react in a timely fashion will suffer losses; those who are alert to the market, and who are quick to act, will be rewarded with profits. Self-interest, not your haranguing memos and phone calls, will efficiently, effectively, and expeditiously disseminate all relevant information in a free market economy. Depend on it. Self-interest works better than command and control.

PRIME MINISTER: But wouldn't everyone need an advanced degree in economics in order to process these price signals, to make the computations you describe, and to follow the intersections, tangencies, and shifting points of equilibrium in your notorious economic graphs? With all due respect, I must say that given the economists I've had to deal with, I find a nation of

Ph.D.s in economics to be a frightening prospect! As I recall, it was Walter Bagehot, the nineteenth-century English business writer, who quipped that no true Englishman in his secret soul was ever sorry to read the obituary of an economist.[7]

ADVISOR: Having been surrounded myself by thousands of economists at the annual meetings of the American Economic Association, I, too, would find the prospect alarming. Fortunately, it is not necessary. As Professor Friedman explains, the appropriate analogy is that of a top-flight billiard player. Champion pool players need not have any formal education in the theorems of advanced trigonometry in order to ply their craft. They calculate their angles of impact and deflection *as if* they understood trigonometry, and make their shots *as if* they were applying trigonometry to the pool table, even though the concepts of sine, cosine, arc, and tangent may be completely alien to them. Trigonometric analysis is merely a formal apparatus for describing what the expert billiard player does by instinct.[8]

PRIME MINISTER: To paraphrase Molière's Bourgeois Gentleman, the billiard player is a trigonometrist but doesn't know it. In the same way, your free market businesspeople are economists without knowing it?

ADVISOR: Precisely.

PRIME MINISTER: How can you be so sure that these businesspeople/economists will react properly to the information conveyed by prices? After all, reacting is one thing; reacting correctly is quite another.

---

[7] Quoted in Douglas A. Irwin, ed., *Jacob Viner: Essays on the Intellectual History of Economics* (Princeton, N.J.: Princeton University Press, 1991), 238.

[8] Milton Friedman, *Essays in Positive Economics* (Chicago: University of Chicago Press, 1953), 21–23.

ADVISOR: Losses play the pivotal role. A private firm that fails to react correctly to these price signals will lose money. Its losses will force it to change its ways. It has no choice: it must either recognize and correct its mistake or go out of business. This may be harsh for the individuals and firms involved. But it is highly beneficial for the society at large, because it ensures that resources will flow into the hands of those able to use them most effectively.[9] In a centrally controlled economy, by contrast, it is obvious that waste is built into the system: No enterprise director is constrained by a bottom line; no director faces the specter of bankruptcy if the cost of production exceeds the value of the product; and directors obtain subsidies from the state to bail out their operations. The reason economic freedom works is that it does not tolerate mistakes.

PRIME MINISTER: Your government's habit of bailing out corporate giants—direct bailouts of the Chrysler Corporation, Lockheed Corporation, and Continental Illinois Bank variety, as well as indirect bailouts via government restraints on import competition, tax privileges, and loan favors, compensated cost overruns, and juggled defense contracts—seems to refute your theory, however.[10] It suggests that some firms are perceived to be too big to be allowed to fail—that the "market" rules governing them are radically different from those under which smaller firms must operate. It suggests economic Darwinism in reverse—survival of the *least*

---

[9] Milton Friedman and Rose Friedman, *Tyranny of the Status Quo* (New York: Harcourt, Brace Jovanovich, 1984), 49, 121–22.

[10] For a general analysis, see Walter Adams and James W. Brock, "Corporate Bigness and the Bailout Factor," *Journal of Economic Issues* 20 (Dec. 1986): 919–40.

fit, provided they are big enough and incompetent enough. One might say that some of your industrial giants survive not because they are better but because they are bigger, not because they are fitter but because they are fatter.

ADVISOR: I vehemently opposed the government bailouts of Chrysler, Lockheed, and Continental Illinois. I testified before Congress against each of them, in the strongest, most emphatic terms possible.

PRIME MINISTER: Your failure to carry the day must be a tribute to the political firepower deployed against you.

ADVISOR: It was brutal. Chief executives, labor union chiefs, workers, suppliers, subcontractors, mayors, governors, senators, representatives, Republicans and Democrats—day after day an unrelenting army of lobbyists descended on Congress and the President demanding government rescue.

PRIME MINISTER: The political economy of massive firm size seems to have triumphed over your economic logic.

ADVISOR: Of course, your economy is not immune from the problem either. I believe you refer to it as the "soft budget constraint"—the problem of state-guaranteed survival of enterprises, regardless of their economic performance.[11]

PRIME MINISTER: Perhaps our economies have more in common than you suspect. But enough of theory. Let's turn to practical policy recommendations. In order to introduce the market price system and make it work,

[11] János Kornai, "The Soft Budget Constraint," *Kyklos* 39 (1986): 3–30.

what steps should we take? Where should we begin? What should we do?

ADVISOR: The answer is simple. You must abolish centralized government control of prices throughout your economy. You must liberate prices, and allow them to be freely determined through the interaction of the forces of demand and supply we've just discussed. You must enable producers to determine prices on their own, without government interference. You must eliminate state subsidies for enterprises. In short, you must get government out of the way, and allow the free market price system to perform its economic work.[12]

PRIME MINISTER: Surely you're not serious! What you are advocating would ignite skyrocketing price inflation: Our state has held prices low for decades; a sudden and precipitate abolition of these state controls and subsidies would trigger an explosion of prices that our people could not bear.

ADVISOR: If you're going to cut a dog's tail off, don't do it by inches. Do it swiftly with a single stroke. Sure, there will be some difficulty. But not for long. As soon as your people become convinced that this is a one-shot price spike, things will settle down.[13]

PRIME MINISTER: Some difficulty? For a short time? Price liberalization by Latin American nations during the 1970s generated huge price inflations for four to

---

[12] David Lipton and Jeffrey Sachs, "Creating a Market Economy in Eastern Europe: The Case of Poland," *Brookings Papers on Economic Activity* 1 (1990): 100; Alfred E. Kahn and Merton J. Peck, "Price Deregulation, Corporatization, and Competition," in Merton J. Peck and Thomas J. Richardson, eds., *What Is to Be Done? Proposals for the Soviet Transition to the Market* (New Haven: Yale University Press, 1991).

[13] David Lipton and Jeffrey Sachs, "Poland's Economic Reform," *Foreign Affairs* 69 (Summer 1990):58.

five years, after which their prices continued to rise by 40–150 percent annually.[14] In Yugoslavia, price decontrol triggered an inflation rate of 457 percent. [*Flipping to another chart*] As for Poland, just look at Chart 3— removal of controls produced price hikes exceeding 2,000 percent.[15] In the former Soviet Union, decontrol in January 1992 produced immediate price hikes of 350 percent, with food prices shooting up by three, four, ten times or more.[16] What you are proposing is "catastroika," not perestroika![17]

ADVISOR: I don't believe that what you're describing is really as inflationary as you imply. As I said before, if the official prices for goods are low, but the goods aren't available in the stores, then low prices really don't exist. If you wanted a new car, you had to wait three to four years in Czechoslovakia, and as much as six years in Hungary and Poland.[18] If you must spend hours waiting in line to purchase something, then its price isn't low—you're just paying with standing hours instead of work hours. What good are cheap prices if the goods aren't available? In a price-decontrolled economy, temporary inflation induces a greater supply of goods, eliminates your notorious queues and shortages, and

[14] Alejandro Foxley, *Latin American Experiments in Neoconservative Economics* (Berkeley, Cal.: University of California Press, 1983), 121.

[15] Jackson Diehl, "The Perils of Price Reform," *Washington Post* (*Weekly Edition*), Oct. 24–30, 1988, 8–9; Dariusz K. Rosati, "Poland: Systemic Reforms and Economic Policy in the 1980s," in George Blazyca and Ryszard Rapacki, eds., *Poland into the 1990s: Economy and Society in Transition* (London: Pinter Publishers, 1991), 29.

[16] Bohlen, "Russians Put Anxiety Aside and Try to Eke Out a Living," *New York Times*, Mar. 1, 1992, 1.

[17] Philip Hanson, "Soviet Economic Reform: Perestroika or 'Catastroika'?" *World Policy Journal*, 8 (Spring 1991):289.

[18] János Kornai, *The Socialist System*, 236.

CHART 3. "BIG BANG" INFLATION RATE IN POLAND,
JANUARY 1989–AUGUST 1990

| | | Inflation Rate | |
| | | December | Previous |
Year	Month	1988 = 100	month = 100
1989	January	111.0	111.0
	February	119.8	107.9
	March	129.5	108.1
	April	142.2	109.8
	May	152.4	107.2
	June	161.7	106.1
	July	177.1	109.5
	August	247.1	139.5
	September	331.9	134.4
	October	513.6	154.8
	November	628.5	122.4
	December	739.8	117.7
1990	January	1,328.6	179.6
	February	1,644.8	123.8
	March	1,715.6	104.3
	April	1,844.2	107.5
	May	1,929.1	104.6
	June	1,994.7	103.4
	July	2,066.5	103.6
	August	2,103.7	101.8

Source: Adapted from Roman Frydman and Stanislaw Wellisz, "The Ownership-Control Structure and the Behavior of Polish Enterprises during the 1990 Reforms," in Vittorio Corbo, Fabrizio Coricelli, and Jan Bossak, eds., Reforming Central and Eastern European Economies (Washington, D.C.: World Bank, 1991), 144.

thus represents a *rise* in the people's standard of living.[19]

PRIME MINISTER: Nightingales don't feed on fairy tales! I'm afraid you are too much of an academic theorist,

---

[19] Lipton and Sachs, "Creating a Market Economy," 79.

and not practical enough.[20] Let's look at the facts with common sense. At current wages and private market prices, a typical Muscovite would have to work 750 hours to pay for a pair of women's dress shoes, 500 hours to pay for a pair of men's dress shoes, 750 hours to afford a woman's skirt, and nearly a week to buy a mere pound of smoked sausage.[21] The daily per capita cost of the standard grocery basket rose 1,100 percent between April and December 1991; the price of a cubic meter of lumber rose 900 percent. The real wages of perhaps as many as 90 percent of the Russian people may now be below the subsistence level.[22]

ADVISOR: But examine the facts further. In the case of Poland, prices did explode—initially. However, the inflation rate subsequently declined substantially, from a monthly rate of 80 percent in January 1990 to a monthly rate of 5 percent by the following April–July period. More important, goods have become more widely available while queues and shortages have begun to diminish significantly.[23]

PRIME MINISTER: Before, prices were low, and products were in short supply. Now, goods are more plentiful, but no one can afford them. What's the difference? Western economists sometimes forget that the majority of our

[20] See "A Pragmatist's Approach to the Soviet Economy: A Conversation with Nikolai Shmelev and Ed A. Hewett," *Brookings Review,* Winter 1989/90, 27–32.

[21] *New York Times,* Jan. 2, 1992, A6.

[22] Bohlen, "Russians Put Anxiety Aside"; Laurie Hays, "Russia Yielding on Its Policy of Tight Money," *Wall Street Journal,* Mar. 20, 1992, A8; *Current Digest of the Soviet Press,* Feb. 5, 1992, 34.

[23] Olivier Blanchard et al., *Reform in Eastern Europe* (Cambridge, Mass.: MIT Press, 1991), 18; Lipton and Sachs, "Poland's Economic Reform," 56; id., "Creating a Market Economy," 119.

people already live at the barest margin of survival. Ours is not an affluent society like yours, in which such hardship could be absorbed without pushing people into literal starvation. The Soviet standard of living in 1988 was two thousand dollars per capita annually—a mere tenth that of the United States.[24] At open market exchange rates, Soviet per capita income may have fallen to as little as eight dollars per month, and some people openly refer to Boris Yeltsin as "the tsar of beggars and thieves." Russian leaders are beginning to fear a "revolt by the naked."[25] Wouldn't it be more practical to decontrol prices gradually rather than all at once? Isn't it possible to create capitalism with a human face?

ADVISOR: You can't cross a chasm in two jumps.[26] Piecemeal price decontrol would inevitably become politicized. Each phased price increase would become embroiled in parliamentary debate. The unpopularity of price rises would ensure that each step toward decontrol would be too little too late. The result would be refusals to sell, panic buying and hoarding, and continued obstruction of normal trade channels, all of which would discredit and undermine your efforts to restructure. It would also tend to instill expectations of future inflation, thereby rendering control of inflation even more difficult to achieve in the long run.[27]

---

[24] Measured by gross domestic price (GDP) per capita. Economist, *Book of Vital World Statistics* (New York: Times Books, 1990), 40.

[25] "Russia Yielding on Its Policy of Tight Money," *Wall Street Journal*, Mar. 20, 1992, A8; *Current Digest of the Soviet Press* 62, no. 40 (1990): 29.

[26] Jeffrey Sachs, quoted in George M. Taber, "Rx for Russia: Shock Therapy," *Time*, Jan. 27, 1992, 37.

[27] Alfred E. Kahn and Merton J. Peck, "Price Deregulation, Corporatization, and Competition," in Merton J. Peck and Thomas J. Richardson, eds.,

PRIME MINISTER: Single leaps across chasms sound spectacular. But it is only in Hollywood movies that the hero always makes it to the other side. The alternative is to try to build a bridge across the canyon—admittedly a slower, less dramatic approach, but surely safer and more workable.[28]

I invite your attention to the Chinese policy of gradual economic liberalization, described as "crossing the river by feeling the stones underfoot." China's real GNP has increased 9 percent annually for the past fourteen years; cotton output has tripled; consumption of seafood, pork, and poultry has doubled or even quadrupled; the number of washing machines per hundred households has risen from six to more than eighty; and real incomes in the countryside have tripled. In short, the Chinese model, where an authoritarian government promotes a market economy in cautious, carefully controlled doses, seems to work.[29]

ADVISOR: I must remind you of the Russian proverb: If trees are to be cut, then wood chips must fly.

PRIME MINISTER: These are not wood chips we're dealing with. These are people struggling to survive—citizens capable of inciting political insurrection. To return to inflation, would it not be a likely outcome of

---

What Is to Be Done? Proposals for the Soviet Transition to the Market (New Haven: Yale University Press, 1991).

[28] Padma Desai, *Perestroika in Perspective* (Princeton, N.J.: Princeton University Press, 1990), 179.

[29] "Survey of China," Economist, Nov. 28, 1992 S3–4. See also Stanislaw Gomulka, Yong-Chool Ha, and Cae-One Kim, *Economic Reforms in the Socialist World* (Armonk, N.Y.: M. E. Sharpe, 1989), 9–55. For an argument in favor of a gradualist economic transformation program for Hungary, see Paul Hare and Tamás Révész, "Hungary's Transition to the Market: The Case Against a 'Big Bang'," *Economic Policy*, Apr. 1992, 228–56.

price decontrol that our liberated enterprises would simply raise their prices, leading our workers to demand higher wages, which in turn would generate rising enterprise costs and another round of increases in product prices? We've seen this happen many times already.[30] Wouldn't price decontrol simply unleash a spiraling price-wage-price inflation? John Kenneth Galbraith argues that even in your own advanced market system, this problem is endemic since the market power of labor unions to raise wages coalesces with the market power of large firms to pass on higher labor costs through increases in product prices. He argues that the problem can be resolved only through some form of selective, government-imposed price and wage controls. According to Galbraith, the failure of your macroeconomists to confront this problem has rendered their debates enchantingly inconsequential.[31]

ADVISOR: The only way to achieve a free market is to make it free, not to hobble it first, and then remove the hobbles. Price and wage controls are counterproductive. They distort the price structure, subvert the working of the market system, and waste resources in the effort required to construct and enforce them, as well as the inevitable counterefforts to evade them. Distortions accumulate, suppressed inflationary pressures reach the boiling point, adverse consequences steadily worsen, and the entire program eventually collapses.[32]

[30] Diehl, "Perils of Price Reform."

[31] John Kenneth Galbraith, *The New Industrial State*, 2d ed., rev. (Boston: Houghton Mifflin, 1971), 249–62; testimony of John Kenneth Galbraith, U.S. Congress, Joint Economic Committee, *Hearings: The 1971 Midyear Review of the Economy*, 92d Cong., 1st sess., 1971, 72–77.

[32] Friedman and Friedman, *Free to Choose*, 267–68.

PRIME MINISTER: So government price controls are removed, and what do enterprises do? Do they play the competitive market game you describe? No! They conspire to fix their own prices! When the former Soviet republics decontrolled bread prices in early 1992, for example, producers decided that if the state would no longer control prices, they would. And so they did—raising them more than threefold. Like your nineteenth-century robber barons, producers across the board are colluding to control markets.[33]

ADVISOR: What you are referring to is the problem of monopoly pricing power, a situation where there is no effective competition. I suggest we tackle this topic, and the larger challenge of demonopolizing your economy, after bracing ourselves with dinner and a good night's rest.

PRIME MINISTER: Good suggestion. Would you care for a vodka?

ADVISOR: I thought you'd never ask.

PRIME MINISTER: Na zdorovye!

[33] Laurie Hays and Adi Ignatius, "Moscow's 'Capitalists' Decide the Best Price Is a Firmly Fixed One," *Wall Street Journal*, Jan. 21, 1992, 1.

Day 3 – The Monopoly Dilemma

Monopoly pricing power poses a dilemma. The conferees discuss communist gigantomania and capitalist cartels, free trade, mergers and conglomeration, and rule-of-law versus regulatory and structural remedies from the perspective of the contestable markets theory.

PRIME MINISTER: Yesterday, you carefully explained the role of prices in a market economy. You made a case for entrusting the determination of prices to the untrammeled interaction of supply and demand rather than to the administrative discretion of a command-and-control bureaucracy. You advocated prompt, across-the-board decontrol of prices as an indispensable step in our transition to a market economy.

ADVISOR: Quite so. In a market economy, competition is the harness that makes self-interest work. The core of competition is the existence of a sufficient number of sellers independently offering choices to buyers, or standing ready to do so. To make sales, producers must then outdo their active and potential rivals in quality and price. Buyers can protect themselves against sellers who charge exorbitant prices or offer deficient quality by turning to alternative sellers or to potential newcomers. Success thus depends upon efficient production of goods and services that consumers or business buyers want, along with aggressive pricing at levels consistent with efficient costs. Success goes to those who risk their efforts and capital to invest in creating more desirable choices for tomorrow.

PRIME MINISTER: I am afraid that is an idealized version of the market economy. Yet I have the uncomfortable feeling that a transition to your system will not be as easy and as frictionless as you suggest. What is obvious in theory is often difficult to translate into practice.

ADVISOR: I don't understand your reservations.

PRIME MINISTER: I think you will agree that markets work efficiently only if they satisfy certain structural preconditions. Supply and demand will operate in the public interest only in a competitive framework—if there are no barriers to the entry of newcomers, if there is no collusion among sellers (or among buyers), and if firms do not wield monopoly power over markets. In the absence of these conditions, that is in the absence of meaningful competition, markets will not yield socially desirable results.

ADVISOR: You have just stated a truism.

PRIME MINISTER: But this is the nub of the problem in the economies of Eastern Europe. Our major manufacturing industries are totally devoid of competition. Our industrial landscapes are densely populated with giant monopolies, linked with one another in a vertically integrated, hierarchical chain. Their market position is insulated from potential challenge by both domestic and foreign rivals. As the only producers in their assigned fiefdoms, they exercise absolute, arbitrary dominance over their hapless customers. And, as wards of the state, they are protected from failure.

ADVISOR: Only a gradual weakening and, ultimately, a total elimination of the manufacturers' monopoly will result in anything new. Consumers need to have rights and opportunities to take what is offered or turn it down. That means they have to have a real choice. And producers must be faced with the real possibility of loss and even total bankruptcy if the goods they produce cannot be sold.

PRIME MINISTER: Under prevailing conditions, such rules of the game are almost impossible to enforce. Our economies currently have a whopping excess of demand over supply. Inflation is pervasive and pernicious. There are massive shortages of all types of goods. Entry into fields dominated by giant state enterprises is formidable, if not impossible. And foreign competition, at least for the moment, is weak, not to say anemic.

ADVISOR: That is the price you are paying for decades of socialism. Socialist management—or, more precisely, mismanagement—has produced a distorted world. Factories are too large and employ far too many people. They are located in the wrong places. They produce the wrong products, using the wrong technologies. They are organized the wrong way. The whole structure is wrong, compared to what it would have been if market forces had been allowed to operate. Not surprisingly, concentration ratios are inordinately high, and plants are excessively large—[*flipping to Chart 4*] just look at these Soviet concentration statistics! It is a case of gigantomania run amok.

PRIME MINISTER: Unfortunately, we don't have the option of choosing a better history. Engels told us that socialism was a single giant factory. Lenin was a devout admirer of your giant, turn-of-the-century capitalist monopolies. He regarded them as superior economic organisms exemplifying Darwinian survival of the fittest. He believed that monopolies, trusts, and cartels perfected modern mass production techniques and raised them to their highest stage of development.

CHART 4. SOVIET MONOPOLIES, 1990

Product	Producer	Percent of Total Soviet Production
Consumer goods		
Sewing machines	Shveinaya Association, Podolsk	100
Washing machines	Elektrobytpribor Factory, Kirov	90
Transport		
Trolley buses	Uritsky Factory, Engels	97
Forklift trucks	Autopogruzhxhik Association, Kharkov	87
Diesel locomotives	Industrial Association, Voroshilovgrad	95
Electric locomotives and trains	Electric Locomotive Plant, Novocherkassk	70
Tram rails	Integrated Steel Works, Kuznetsk	100
Metals		
Reinforced steel	Krivoy-Rog-stal, Krivoy Rog	55
Construction equipment		
Concrete mixers	Integrated Mill, Tuva Works	93
Road-building cranes	Sverdlovsk Plant, Sverdlovsk	75
Locomotive cranes	Engineering Plant, Kirov	100
Oil, chemicals, and chemical engineering equipment		
Polypropylene	Neftkhimichesky Combine, Perm	73

CHART 4 (CONTINUED)

Product	Producer	Percent of Total Soviet Production
Sucker rods for deep oil wells	Ochesk Engineering Plant, Ochesk	87
Hoists for coal mines	City Coal Machinery Plant, Donetsk	100
Coking equipment	Kopeisk Engineering Plant, Chelyabinsk	100

Source: Adapted from "The Best of All Monopoly Profits," *Economist,* Aug. 11, 1990, 67.

What he admired especially was their superior planning capacity; in his opinion, they embodied modern, rational production. The wise policy, he believed, was not to resist concentration of industry, but to promote it, which he and Stalin did by "liquidating" small firms, and consolidating them into centrally administered giants. Mergers, monopoly, and market concentration, Lenin often said, were essential building blocks for socialism.[1]

ADVISOR: Lenin distrusted market forces, much as the Devil shies away from incense.

PRIME MINISTER: Incense or not, the result is an economic system honeycombed with monopolies and near-monopolies. In the former Soviet Union, for example, 30 to 40 percent of total industrial output comprises

[1] See the excellent account and analysis by Leon M. Herman, "The Cult of Bigness in Soviet Economic Planning," in U.S. Congress, Senate, Committee on the Judiciary, *Hearings on Economic Concentration,* 90th Cong., 2d sess., 1969, pt. 7A, 4346–53; and Alec Nove, An Economic History of the USSR (London, Penguin, 1969).

CHART 5. DISTRIBUTION OF INDUSTRIES BY
CONCENTRATION: SOVIET UNION AND
UNITED STATES, 1980s

| Market Share of | Percent of All Industries | |
Largest Firm(s)*	Soviet Union	United States
0–50	39.2	72.6
50–75	24.1	21.3
75–100	36.6	6.1

Source: Adapted from Merton J. Peck and Thomas J. Richardson, eds.,
What Is to Be Done? Proposals for the Soviet Transition to the Market
(New Haven: Yale University Press, 1991), 65.
*Soviet Union: market share of single largest firm; United States:
market share of four largest firms.

products for which there is but a single manufacturer.[2]
In eighty-three of the country's most important product lines, a single enterprise has an absolute monopoly.
In eighty-five product lines, two enterprises control the
entire output. In forty-three product lines, three enterprises. In twenty-eight product lines, four enterprises [*Flipping to another chart*]. For your information,
I have prepared Chart 5 to illustrate the pervasiveness
of monopoly and oligopoly. This, incidentally, is the situation not only in Russia but also in the other nations
of Eastern Europe. [*Flipping to the next chart*] I have
also prepared Chart 6 to show the overwhelming percentages of Soviet workers employed in giant monopolies and oligopolies—underscoring the stupendous
problems of privatization.

[2] *The Economy of the USSR: Summary and Recommendations* (Washington, D.C.: International Monetary Fund, 1990), 26.

CHART 6. PERCENTAGE DISTRIBUTION OF INDUSTRIAL
WORKFORCE BY FIRM SIZE IN THE UNITED STATES AND
SOVIET UNION, C. 1990

	Percent of Industrial Workforce	
Firm Size	United States	Soviet Union
1–499 employees	61.4	15.0
500–999 employees	12.7	11.7
1,000 or more employees	25.8	73.3

Source: Adapted from Stanley Fischer, "Stabilization and Economic Reform in Russia," *Brookings Papers on Economic Activity* 1 (1992): 95.
Note: Some percentages do not total 100 because of rounding.

ADVISOR: I imagine that these concentration statistics understate the true extent of monopoly power. They show only the share of total national output controlled by a single producer or a group of dominant producers. Thus, they tend to exaggerate the number of potentially competing sellers in markets that are not nationwide but local or regional. For example, while the former Soviet Union had more than five hundred footwear producers, each factory was exclusively oriented to servicing the needs of a particular region.[3] This problem was particularly pronounced for such products as cement, where transportation costs are significant.[4]

PRIME MINISTER: The results of monopoly power, as economic theory tells us, are predictable. Once the monopolist is liberated from price controls, it will charge

[3] V. Tsapelik and A. Yakovlev, "Monopoly in the Soviet Economy," *Problems of Economics* 34 (May 1991): 35.
[4] Alfred E. Kahn and Merton J. Peck, "Price Deregulation, Corporatization, and Competition," in Merton J. Peck and Thomas J. Richardson, eds., *What Is to Be Done? Proposals for the Soviet Transition to the Market* (New Haven: Yale University Press, 1991), 66.

what the traffic will bear. Sometimes it will ignore the dictates of rational profit maximization and charge more than that. Take the case of the giant Roselmash enterprise in Rostov, which is Russia's only producer of harvester combines. It's a terribly inefficient factory, which turns out more harvesters than all U.S. producers put together. When prices were decontrolled in January 1992, this enterprise decided to jack up prices by 1,500 percent while at the same time increasing the salaries of its management and employees. The result was that nobody would buy harvesters—or, to be more accurate, could afford to buy harvesters. With virtually no sales, the enterprise is now near bankruptcy and pleading with the state to save it.[5]

ADVISOR: This is not a new phenomenon. More than two hundred years ago, Adam Smith wrote in *The Wealth of Nations*: "The price of monopoly is upon every occasion the highest which can be got. The natural price, or the price under free competition, on the contrary, is the lowest which can be taken, not upon every occasion, indeed, but for any considerable time together. The one is upon every occasion the highest which can be squeezed out of the buyers, or which, it is supposed, they will consent to give: The other is the lowest which the sellers can commonly afford to take, and at the same time continue their business" (p. 61).

PRIME MINISTER: Breaking up such monopolistic enterprises will be one of the most difficult challenges in our transition to a market economy. We can't just wave a magic wand to create a second manufacturer of harvesters overnight, even though the monopolist con-

---

[5] *Washington Post Weekly Edition*, April 13–19, 1992, 8.

tinues to enjoy—and abuse—undue economic power. Unfortunately, the situation is just as bad, or nearly so, in many industries in our region. Take the VAZ Auto Works in Russia, for example. One day after prices were deregulated, VAZ announced price hikes of 750 percent. Management's rationale was straightforward: "Ten million people are bidding for the 700,000 cars we produce annually, and among these people, more than enough can afford to pay the higher prices. Some even travel thousands of miles to our factory in hopes of somehow snagging cars before they are shipped to customers who signed up for them years ago." Why not, then, raise output so that the ten million potential customers can buy vehicles without having to wait so long? "Satisfying demand by increasing production," said the management, "would make buyers less willing to pay high prices. Our current profit margin is 33 percent per vehicle. Increased production would threaten this profit by chipping away at the price. Lower prices would force us to cut costs which would mean shrinking our labor force of more than 200,000 people. While we still have the opportunity, we choose the easier way. We maintain profits by raising prices rather than reducing costs."[6]

ADVISOR: Don't let such situations persuade you to retain price controls. If you do, you would be blocking the entire process of economic reform.[7]

PRIME MINISTER: So your advice, as they say in Russia, is to let the bear dance while the gypsy takes the money?

---

[6] Louis Uchitelle, "Old Economics of Russian Cars," *New York Times*, Feb. 25, 1992, C2.

[7] Kahn and Peck, "Price Deregulation," 67.

ADVISOR: Not at all. You must remember that, as a general rule, even monopoly prices are preferable to prices controlled by the state. Such prices will clear markets. They will equate supply and demand. In so doing, they will eliminate queues and the incentive to barter. Moreover, although monopoly prices are higher than competitive prices, they are held in check by the profit maximization motive. After all, even monopolists cannot be unconcerned about exceeding the point at which higher prices so discourage consumption that they reduce profits. Nor, in an open economy, can monopolists ignore the danger that excessive prices, poor quality, or poor service will attract competitors. Besides, monopolies tend to be transitory and temporary.[8]

PRIME MINISTER: Why, then, would Václav Klaus, the former finance minister of Czechoslovakia and a leader of the free market movement in our region, insist that we take steps to increase competition before lifting price controls. "The mistake," he says, "is to begin price reform with a monopolistic structure." Nikolai Petrakov, the distinguished Russian economist agrees. He asserts that "the first thing to do before deregulating prices is to create the right conditions for competition, without which there can be no price freedom. One of the first measures to be taken is therefore to demonopolize our economy, which is the most highly monopolized in the world."[9] It hardly seems prudent

---

[8] Ibid., 68; Lipton and Sachs, "Creating a Market Economy," 100–101.

[9] Klaus's statement appeared in Steven Greenhouse, "Poland Applies Shock Treatment to Revive Its Economy," *New York Times*, Feb. 12, 1990, C9. Petrakov's statement appeared in *Le Monde*, Mar. 25, 1990, 1, 41. See also Martin C. Spechler, "Competition and Structural Change in Eastern Europe," *Review of Industrial Organization* 6 (1991): 189–98.

to replace state monopolies with unregulated private monopolies.

ADVISOR: On his trip to China, Professor Friedman was asked whether he will still put his faith in the market even in situations where there is no competition. "You're asking," he replied, "which of two bad things is worse: If you can have government monopoly or private monopoly, which would you rather have? I don't like either, but I would rather have private monopoly for two reasons. First and most important: because it's easier to break down a private monopoly than a government monopoly; because a private monopoly does not have the power to keep reaching, and reaching, and reaching. If there had been a government monopoly in the United States for making coaches pulled by horses, the development of the automobile would have been prevented. But if there had been a private monopoly in those carriages, the development of the automobile would still have gone on. In that respect, therefore, the private monopoly is less damaging than the government monopoly. In addition, there is one general rule: nobody spends somebody else's money as carefully as he spends his own. So, as the monopolist is spending his own money when he produces products, he tends to be more efficient than the government enterprise, which is spending somebody else's money."[10]

PRIME MINISTER: It is a fine chapel, the Czechs would say, but where are the saints?

ADVISOR: Don't underestimate the power of competition and don't overestimate the permanence of monopoly.

---

[10] Milton Friedman, *Friedman in China* (Hong Kong: Chinese University Press, 1990), 119. See also Kahn and Peck, "Price Deregulation," 68.

Monopoly is subject to erosion—what Schumpeter called "the gale of creative destruction." In the long run, dynamic changes are highly likely to undermine monopolies wherever they exist. And even in the short run, there is generally a wider range of substitutes than there seems to be at first blush. Hence private enterprises are fairly limited in the extent to which it is profitable to keep prices above cost.[11] Moreover, our experience in the United States has shown that government regulatory agencies that were set up to control monopolies have often tended themselves to fall under the control of the producers, with the result that prices have often not been any lower with regulation than without regulation.[12]

PRIME MINISTER: Are you saying that, in some sense, all markets are competitive in the long run, and that there is therefore no need to regulate monopolies?

ADVISOR: Yes. In fact, there is a new theory—the contestable markets theory—which holds that potential entry into, or competition for, the market disciplines behavior almost as effectively as would actual competition within the market. Thus, even if a market is dominated by a single firm, it is contestable and will perform in a competitive fashion.[13]

PRIME MINISTER: [*After conversing with a deputy*] Another excellent theory that fails in practice. In the U.S. domestic airline industry, for example, a series of megamergers following deregulation and the concomitant

---

[11] Kahn and Peck, "Price Deregulation," 68.

[12] Milton Friedman, *Capitalism and Freedom*, (Chicago: University of Chicago Press, 1962), 128–29.

[13] Elizabeth Bailey, "Contestability and the Design of Regulatory and Antitrust Policy," American Economic Review 71 (May 1981): 178.

increase in concentration resulted in significant fare increases and a noticeable deterioration of service. After acquiring Ozark, for example, TWA discontinued forty flights out of St. Louis, and raised fares by as much as 33 percent. And now at eighteen hubs where a single airline controls 50 percent or more of the traffic, originating passengers are forced to pay significantly higher fares—in some cases over 50 percent more—compared to standard levels. It is a fine outcome when the public pays more and more for less and less.

ADVISOR: The purpose of airline deregulation in the United States was to allow free market forces to determine the best economic organization of the industry. Whenever and wherever there is a profitable opportunity in a deregulated airline market, an entrant need merely fly its airplane into the airport, undercut the incumbent's price, and fly the route profitably. Should the incumbent retaliate with a sharp price cut, the entrepreneur will fly its airplane away to exploit some other lucrative opportunity. Clearly, the U.S. airline industry is a perfect example of how the contestable market theory works.

PRIME MINISTER: Of course, this assumes that the new entrants can get landing gates or buy them from the very airlines whose position they are trying to undermine—and that they can gain equal and nondiscriminatory access to the computerized reservation systems controlled by their major competitors. Besides, in most industries, capital is not as mobile as in the airline industry. You can't move a steel mill or an auto plant from one location to another with the same insouciance as you can change the flight pattern of an airline. But let us leave the U.S. situation aside. Where is the new entry going to come from in the case of Eastern Europe with its pervasively monopolized industries?

ADVISOR: Some entry could come from indigenous sources. Under Communist rule, enterprises were highly specialized and often restricted to a single product line. Earlier, you mentioned VAZ, the giant automobile company in the former Soviet Union. It controls 58 percent of total output. But there are other Russian car companies, each manufacturing a single model, directed at a particular stratum of the market. ZIL, for example, manufactures only large limousines. As in the West, these smaller companies, once free and motivated to do so, could exploit the potential production and marketing economies and opportunities for profit by broadening their product lines, thereby challenging VAZ itself.[14] The same can happen in the field of textile fibers. Currently, of the 375 different fibers, 288 are produced by a single monopoly enterprise. There is no reason why some of these enterprises cannot broaden their product lines and engage in competition on a broad scale.

PRIME MINISTER: Any other sources of potential entry?

ADVISOR: There is, of course, foreign competition. This is perhaps the best antimonopoly policy. In the United States, for example, automobile imports in the last few years have amounted to roughly 30 percent of the domestic market. They have been a major factor in undermining the erstwhile dominance of the Big Three

---

[14] Kahn and Peck, "Price Deregulation," 70.

and the primary source of competition in price and product quality.[15]

PRIME MINISTER: If foreign competition has these beneficial effects, why has your government imposed import quotas on automobiles for the last twelve years? Why has it restricted steel imports into an oligopolized domestic market for more than twenty years? Why does it still have bilateral agreements with some twenty-four countries to limit steel exports to the United States? For that matter, why does it think its interest in protective tariffs outweighs its proclaimed interest in helping our struggling new states, with the erstwhile Bush administration proposing a punitive tariff on uranium imported into the United States from the former Soviet republics[16] and the U.S. government imposing a stiff tariff on Goya cheese from Hungary?

ADVISOR: More often than not, such restraints on competition are politically motivated. They are good politics and bad economics.

PRIME MINISTER: What makes you think that the countries of Eastern Europe are any less vulnerable to political pressures than the United States or the European Community? You and I know that our monopoly enterprises are huge, inefficient, technologically backward dinosaurs. Once exposed to international competition, many, if not most of them, are bound to fail. And when they do, that means unemployment for millions of people. How can our fledgling governments possibly survive and continue with their plans for

---

[15] Ibid., 74.

[16] Keith Bradsher, "Ex-Soviet States Face Penalty on Uranium Exports," *New York Times*, May 30, 1992, A1.

a market economy, if international competition produces such catastrophic consequences?

PRIME MINISTER: An ailing patient must be willing to take some
bitter pills.

PRIME MINISTER: It's easier to prescribe bitter pills than
to swallow them. Besides, how do you propose we pay
for the imports that are so crucial in curbing monopoly
power? As the Polish experience demonstrates, imports
will be inordinately expensive at the exchange rates
likely to prevail once our currencies are made freely
convertible.

ADVISOR: That is true, but this in turn will provide an
additional stimulus to competitive domestic manufacture—provided, once again, that all restraints on competitive entry and market interpenetration by domestic
enterprises are removed.[17]

PRIME MINISTER: Those are pretty tall assumptions and,
under current conditions, quite unrealistic. Hope is a
good breakfast but a poor supper. But let us go on. Do
you have any other suggestions for an effective anti-
monopoly policy?

ADVISOR: Once your monopolies are privatized and prices
deregulated—and this must be your first order of business—you must enact laws to stamp out collusion. You
need a law like Section 1 of our Sherman Act, which
prohibits *every* contract, combination, or conspiracy in
restraint of trade.

PRIME MINISTER: Brazil's experience in the summer of
1990 underscores the importance of your point. As
Professor Willig reports, on the very day that the
reform-minded government ended the long-standing

[17] Kahn and Peck, "Price Deregulation," 74.

system of microregulation of milk prices at all stages of distribution, the leadership of the dairy industry declared that if the government would no longer fix their prices, they would have to do it for themselves. After a highly visible public meeting, they decided to award themselves a lucrative raise by setting the newly fixed level of milk prices well above the old one. Within twenty-four hours, de facto price regulation was reinstituted, and the highest levels of government feverishly searched for rules to deal with the situation.[18] When Russia deregulated the price of milk, the instantaneous response of milk producers and distributors was virtually identical to that of their Brazilian counterparts.[19]

ADVISOR: That's an old story. As Adam Smith warned us in *The Wealth of Nations*, "People of the same trade seldom meet together, even for merriment and diversion, but the conversation ends in a conspiracy against the public or some contrivance to raise prices" (p. 128).

PRIME MINISTER: Price conspiracies are not our only problem. Reports from Poland and Hungary tell of conspiracies to prevent newcomers from entering the market, boycotts of firms that do not belong to the conspiracy, and agreements to divide the markets among the conspirators. In some of the former Soviet republics, the cartels are essentially mobsters. They buy up supplies before the goods reach markets in order to pro-

[18] Robert D. Willig, "Anti-Monopoly Policies and Institutions," in Christopher Clague and Gordon C. Rausser, eds., *The Emergence of Market Economies in Eastern Europe* (Oxford: Blackwell, 1992), 187–88.

[19] Laurie Hays and Adi Ignatius, "Half a Loaf: Moscow's 'Capitalists' Decide the Best Price Is a Firmly Fixed One," *Wall Street Journal*, Jan. 21, 1992, A1.

tect fixed prices; interlopers who refuse to accede to cartel terms are swiftly punished, sometimes even murdered in ramshackle hotels catering to merchants and traders.[20]

ADVISOR: Your experience is not unique. In Detroit, for example, members of the auto dealers' cartel have used drive-by shootings to enforce restrictions on the hours that a dealership may stay open. Clearly, the antitrust law I recommend is designed to deal with such situations. The law must prohibit all conspiratorial agreements and combinations that suppress competition or exclude rival enterprises from a fair opportunity to compete. In the United States, that is the function of Section 1 of the Sherman Act.

PRIME MINISTER: What about structural remedies under a new antitrust law? Trustbusting, in other words.

ADVISOR: That would take a long time. The sheer number of enterprises that would have to be broken up in order to create a competitive industrial structure is a formidable obstacle to success. Compounding the already immense task is the indivisibility of many industrial monopolies. Multiplant enterprises or production associations formed from geographically dispersed enterprises are easily divided into separate parts. But what Petrakov calls "organizational monopolies" are physically impossible to break up, because such a monopoly comprises a single giant plant or an enterprise situated on a single site.[21]

PRIME MINISTER: What about mergers? Is an antimerger

---

[20] Igor Reichlin, "Where Cutthroat Competition Means Exactly That," *Business Week*, Mar. 2, 1992, 51.

[21] Heidi Kroll, "Monopoly and Transition to the Market," *Soviet Economy*, 7, no. 2 (1991): 165–66.

law a viable structural policy—one that can be implemented prospectively before monopolies come into being rather after the fact, when it becomes extremely difficult to break them up?

ADVISOR: Some of my colleagues contend that a sound antimerger policy is difficult to design. They say it must be carefully targeted to reach only mergers of monopolistic proportions. Otherwise, it can do more harm than good.

PRIME MINISTER: I am sure you are aware of the lively merger movement in the former Soviet Union. It was actively promoted during the Brezhnev era, and continued later under the guise of perestroika. After 1989, when many government ministries were either liquidated or consolidated, enterprises engaged in similar lines of production were reorganized into "concerns" (*kontserns*), "associations" (*assosiatsyes*), and "consortia" (*konsortsia*). These played the same role as the old ministries and tended to perpetuate, if not exacerbate, the monopolization of industry. When the Ministry of Building Materials was abolished, seven socialist "concerns" were formed from 250 of its formerly subordinate enterprises. These concerns consolidated enterprises producing the same building materials: the cement concern absorbed all cement enterprises, the asbestos concern merged all asbestos combines in the country, and so on. Similarly, five enterprises were allowed to withdraw from the Ministry of Metallurgy to form a nonferrous metals concern. This created an absolute monopoly, which, incidentally, ranked as the largest supplier of nickel in the world.[22] In addition to

[22] Ibid., 155.

these horizontal mergers, many vertical consolidations occurred.

ADVISOR: I wouldn't worry about vertical restructuring.

PRIME MINISTER: Why not? Don't large vertical mergers also subvert competition? Don't they also make for unwarranted concentration of economic power?

ADVISOR: Vertical mergers are a technique for substituting administrative direction for a market transaction. It is a more efficient form of coordination. Vertical integration may cut sales and distribution costs and facilitate the flow of information between different levels of the organization. For example, marketing possibilities may be transmitted more effectively from the retail to the manufacturing level, new product possibilities may be transmitted in the opposite direction, better inventory control may be attained, and better planning of production runs may be achieved. All this creates economies of scale in management.[23]

PRIME MINISTER: I can hardly believe what I am hearing. Your last statement is precisely the argument that communist leaders used to make about the virtues of planning, integration, and coordination. You are not suggesting, are you, that U.S. Steel has to own coal mines in order to produce at the lowest cost? Or that United Airlines should acquire Boeing in order to procure superior planes for its passenger fleet? Or that Consolidated Edison should merge with General Electric to assure itself of an adequate, economical supply of transformers and generators? Is such vertical integration a requirement for efficient performance?

---

[23] Robert Bork, quoted in Walter Adams and James W. Brock, *The Bigness Complex* (New York: Pantheon, 1986), 179–80.

ADVISOR: Such decisions should be left to the market. The market will decide what degree of vertical integration promotes efficiency. In any event, vertical integration has no impact on competition. Competition is an entirely horizontal phenomenon. Moreover, I am sure you are aware that some American economists— John Kenneth Galbraith, for example—would justify substantial firm size on the ground that it performs an indispensable planning function.

PRIME MINISTER: Substantial horizontal size?

ADVISOR: Both horizontal and vertical size. "The size of General Motors," Galbraith wrote, "is in the service not of monopoly or the economies of scale but of planning. And for this planning—control of supply, control of demand, provision of capital, minimization of risk— there is no clear upper limit to the desirable size. The corporate form accommodates to this need. Quite clearly it allows the firm to be very, very large."[24]

PRIME MINISTER: After General Motor's disastrous performance in recent years, I doubt that Professor Galbraith still holds to that view. Nor would he favor the conglomerate mergers that have become so trendy in the communist countries in recent years.

ADVISOR: Conglomerates should be of no concern to you. Radical changes occurred in the science of enterprise management after World War II. The concurrent phenomenal development of electronic computers has promoted and facilitated the expansion of management science. This fundamental development has created opportunities for profits through mergers that remove

[24] John Kenneth Galbraith, *The New Industrial State*, 2d ed. (Boston: Houghton Mifflin, 1971), 76.

assets from the inefficient control of old-fashioned managers and place them under executives schooled in modern management science. Managers are able to control effectively a larger set of activities. Being of general applicability to business operations, management science makes possible reductions in financial and managerial costs and risks through acquisitions of firms in diverse industries. These gains differ markedly from the familiar economies of scale in production, purchasing, or marketing that normally accrue from mergers of firms with related products. Thus the new management science is the primary force behind conglomeration.[25]

PRIME MINISTER: Once again, this argument has a disturbing resemblance to the apologetics that a Soviet economist might advance in defense of the old order. Is it not true that conglomerate power can be used to lessen competition or create monopoly by mobilizing such weapons as cross-subsidization, reciprocal dealing, and competitive forbearance? Is there not a danger, as *Fortune* magazine warned some years ago, that with progressive conglomeration a country might "end up completely dominated by conglomerates happily trading with each other in a new kind of cartel system"?[26]

ADVISOR: Conglomeration—or, as it is sometimes called, aggregate concentration—is not a valid consideration in the formulation of an antitrust policy. As William Baxter, President Reagan's antitrust chief, once explained, "There is nothing written in the sky that says

---

[25] Professor Neil Jacoby, University of California at Los Angeles, 1969 quoted in Adams and Brock, *The Bigness Complex*, 183.
[26] *Fortune*, June 1965, 194.

that the world would not be a perfectly satisfactory place if there were 100 companies, provided each one had 1 percent of every product and service market. In that case there would be extremely high aggregate concentration and, at the same time, perfect competition."[27] When we think of market power, conglomeration is nothing more than an optical illusion.

PRIME MINISTER: But doesn't conglomeration—that is, absolute as distinct from relative firm size—raise serious questions of efficiency?

ADVISOR: In the Western world, conglomerates have come into being because capital markets are an imperfect method for optimizing society's investment decisions and its planning for future output patterns of goods and services. The central planning by conglomerates, as Professor Oliver Williamson notes, is socially beneficial: "First, it is an internal rather than external control mechanism with the constitutional authority and expertise to make detailed evaluations of the performance of each of its operating parts. Second, it can make fine-tuning as well as discrete adjustments. This permits it both to intervene early in a selective, preventative way (a capability which the capital market lacks altogether), as well as to perform *ex post* corrective adjustments, in response to evidence of performance failure, with a surgical precision that the capital market lacks. . . . Finally, the costs of intervention by the general office are relatively low."[28] Thus conglomerates constitute capitalism's creative response

---

[27] *Dun's Review,* Aug. 1981, 38.

[28] Oliver Williamson, *Markets and Hierarchies* (New York: Free Press, 1975), 158–59.

to the evident limits that the capital market experiences in its relations to the firm.

PRIME MINISTER: If my recollection serves me, the great conglomerate merger boom of the 1960s and 1970s was anything but a success in the United States. Giant firms acquired and consolidated hundreds of firms and operations, in wildly unrelated fields, and tried to administer them through vast superstructures of centralized corporate control—much as might a socialist central planning board. IT&T, for example, bought more than 140 companies, producing such diverse products as telephone handsets, battlefield radar, bathroom and kitchen fixtures, automotive brakes, lumber and timber, grass and plant seed, Wonderbread and Hostess Twinkies, fire-extinguishing equipment, air-conditioning apparatus, and books. It also bought companies in such service industries as hotels, auto leasing, and business and technical training schools. The "synergies"—the notion that $2 + 2 = 5$—that these conglomerate bigness complexes were supposed to unleash turned out to be illusory. The Byzantine, ramshackle structures they created became organizational nightmares. They ran aground on the reefs of "reverse synergy"—the reality that sometimes $2 + 2 = 3$. They became, according to *Business Week*, multidivisional, multilocational hydras.[29] They discovered, according to *Fortune*, that the costs of complexity often outweigh the hypothetical cost savings from giant size.[30] I am fascinated—and, frankly, somewhat amused —by the bold new strategy that U.S. conglomerates

[29] Business Week, June 30, 1980, 81.
[30] *Fortune*, Feb. 29, 1988, 36.

have implemented lately: deconglomeration. They are selling off scores of previously acquired businesses, streamlining their operations, and shrinking their size. If efficiency is the goal, the countries of Eastern Europe may be well advised to learn from your experience.

ADVISOR: You are well informed, but I see you haven't learned the basic lesson from that experience: the market works. Managerial mistakes or miscalculations will be punished. If a particular form of organization is efficient, it will thrive. If it isn't, it is doomed to extinction. There is no need for interference by an overly ambitious antitrust authority. In a capitalist economy, resources will naturally flow into the hands of managements that can optimize their use. Superior managements will displace inferior managements as long as the redeployment of resources is not interdicted by government.

PRIME MINISTER: Are you seriously suggesting that the nations recently liberated from central planning embrace such a risky policy?

ADVISOR: Indeed I am, but not until you transfer ownership and control of the giant state enterprises from public to private hands. Massive privatization must be one of the top priorities in your reform agenda for creating a market economy.

PRIME MINISTER: I think that privatization merits a full day's discussion. *Carpe diem.*

ADVISOR: Until tomorrow, *dobre vyetcher*!

Day 4 – Privatization

Privatization is defined as denationalization plus new entrepreneurial ventures. The conferees discuss feedback problems communist-style and capitalist-style, the enormity of the transition, how to let the market value state property and multitudinous ways of transferring it, and obstacles posed by petty crooks and powerful predators.

PRIME MINISTER: Today, let's focus on privatization. We have been bombarded by Western economists armed with their grandiose, multipoint plans, specifying in intricate detail every conceivable procedure and step we should take to restructure our economy. And while these plans differ from one another, all of them assume that we must "privatize" our economic system.

ADVISOR: Yes, that's absolutely essential.

PRIME MINISTER: As you know, our people have been taught for decades to believe that private ownership of the means of production is the root of all evil. Karl Marx vilified private property as an instrument for exploiting workers, for impoverishing, alienating, and degrading them. Marx claimed that individual ownership of the means of production was downright dysfunctional; he considered it one of the key internal contradictions of capitalism, which would culminate in the market system's collapse.

ADVISOR: I've heard that line many times before. As Proudhon put it, "property is theft." The simple fact is that no economic system can provide proper economic incentives unless individuals have the right to buy, own, and sell property as they see fit. Self-interest and voluntary exchanges won't be successful motivators unless there is private ownership of the means of production.[1]

PRIME MINISTER: As the Russian joke has it, under capitalism, one person exploits another; under communism, it is the other way around. What's the difference?

ADVISOR: It's obvious. Even Russian reformers are now embracing the principle that ownership forms the bedrock of legal, institutional, and social relations in the developed world. Only if people are owners, or have that prospect, do they care enough to preserve and maintain property, and to invest time, effort, and money in the hope of future reward. If they hire others to work for them, they have a strong incentive to monitor the workers' behavior; and since the workers know that their employer can reward or fire them, they, too, have a strong incentive to work efficiently.[2] Conversely, a communist economy, lacking private property and its beneficial incentives, suffers from gross waste and inefficiency. It also breeds a phobia against innovation: lacking a profit reward, why should enterprise managers take risks in innovating, when innovating requires new arrangements for supplies, materials, parts, and facilities, when it requires approval from a plethora of planning agencies, and when, if the innovation succeeds, it will only serve to raise future plan targets and

[1] Gary S. Becker, "Why Cold-Turkey Capitalism Would Be Best for the Soviets," *Business Week*, Dec. 24, 1990, 10.

[2] Karen Pennar, "In Russia, a Journey Back to the Future," *Business Week*, Jul. 27, 1992, 49; Milton Friedman, "Market Mechanisms and Central Economic Planning" (G. Warren Nutter Lecture in Political Economy, University of Virginia, 1981), 14.

render them even more difficult to achieve?[3] A typical example is your country's invention back in 1955 of a revolutionary new method for producing paper. Thirty years later, your producers had yet to adopt it, despite its substantial economic and technological advantages.[4]

PRIME MINISTER: But is that any different from the giant firms comprising your own steel oligopoly? Isn't it well documented that for many years they ignored such revolutionary breakthroughs as oxygen furnaces and continuous-casting techniques? Didn't they continue instead to invest millions of dollars in older technologies that were obsolete the moment they were built? As a result, didn't they fall behind the rest of the world?[5] Even today, don't they continue to react to technological advances by producing inch-thick studies "proving" the innovations won't work, even as smaller firms are successfully implementing them?[6] And what about your Big Three automaking firms? Didn't they allow their products and production processes to become antiquated? Didn't they too fall behind the rest of the world?[7]

ADVISOR: That may be. But you can't divorce private ownership of the means of production from the market

[3] Marshall I. Goldman, *USSR in Crisis* (New York: W. W. Norton, 1983), 42–43.

[4] Paul Craig Roberts and Karen LaFollette, *Meltdown: Inside the Soviet Economy* (Washington, D.C.: Cato Institute, 1990), 23.

[5] Walter Adams and Joel B. Dirlam, "Big Steel, Invention, and Innovation," *Quarterly Journal of Economics* 80 (May 1966): 167–89.

[6] Richard Preston, *American Steel* (Englewood Cliffs, N.J.: Prentice Hall, 1991), 12–13; Dana Milbank, "Minimill Inroads in Sheet Market Rouse Big Steel," *Wall Street Journal*, Mar. 9, 1992, B1.

[7] See Walter Adams and James W. Brock, "The Automobile Industry," in Walter Adams, ed., *The Structure of American Industry,* 8th ed. (New York: Macmillan, 1990).

system and the critical function of prices. The motive force of the entire process is the ceaseless search by capitalists to maximize their profits by serving their customers. It is the prospect of private profit that directs production into channels that best serve consumer demand at the least cost. It is private ownership that puts society's resources in the hands of those who best know how to use them. Every step that leads away from private property in production is a step away from rational economic behavior.[8]

PRIME MINISTER: You make it sound so simple. But look at your own corporate form of organization. Ostensibly, the owners of your giant corporations are the stockholders, yes? Yet, typically, there are hundreds of thousands of these individual corporate "owners," spread across your country, and perhaps even around the world. And, isn't such widespread ownership tantamount to "social ownership" of the means of production? When vast segments of your people own a firm, is that really any different from socialism?

ADVISOR: Yes it is, for a critically important reason: Each one of those stockholders can sell his or her share of stock ownership in the corporation. It is their private property, to be kept or disposed of as they wish.

PRIME MINISTER: But isn't there also a separation of ownership from control in your corporate form of organization? As a young student, I read Berle and Means. According to them, if my memory serves me, the stockholders may legally own the corporation, but it is the managers—the presidents, vice presidents, and

[8] Ludwig von Mises, *Socialism: An Economic and Sociological Analysis* (London: Jonathan Cape, 1936), 119, 137–38, 311.

so on—who actually control the corporation's wealth and assets. Didn't Berle and Means argue that this splits the atom of property since the owners don't manage, and the managers aren't the owners? Doesn't this contradict your theory that the quest for profits will spur the owners of industrial property to put it to the most economically efficient use?[9]

ADVISOR: Not at all. If the stockholders are displeased with the management's performance, they can vote to replace the management, or they can sell their shares of stock in the firm, or they can do both. In Hirschman's terminology, they are free to exercise "loyalty, voice, or exit."[10] For example, in what we call the market for corporate control, outsiders like T. Boone Pickens and Carl Icahn can take over a firm by buying a majority of its stock, if they believe the firm is being mismanaged. They can then replace the incumbent managers with a new management team more attentive to stockholder interests.[11]

PRIME MINISTER: The notoriously high bankruptcy rates subsequently suffered by the objects of these takeovers and leveraged buyouts makes me doubt the efficacy of your market for corporate control. The junk bonds used to finance them certainly have lived up to their name.[12]

---

[9] Adolf A. Berle and Gardiner C. Means, *The Modern Corporation and Private Property* (New York: Macmillan, 1932), 8–9.

[10] Albert Hirschman, *Exit, Voice, and Loyalty* (Cambridge, Mass.: Harvard University Press, 1970).

[11] See Henry G. Manne, "Mergers and the Market for Corporate Control," *Journal of Political Economy*, April 1965, 110–20; and the articles by Michael C. Jensen, Gregg A. Jarrell, and F. M. Scherer in *Symposium: Takeovers*, special issue of *Journal of Economic Perspectives*, Winter 1988.

[12] See Walter Adams and James W. Brock, *Antitrust Economics on Trial: A Dialogue on the New Laissez-Faire* (Princeton, N.J.: Princeton University Press, 1991), 96–113.

CHART 7. STATE SECTOR SHARE OF THE
ECONOMY IN SELECTED COMMUNIST AND
CAPITALIST COUNTRIES, MID-1980s (PERCENT)

Czechoslovakia	97.0
East Germany	96.5
Soviet Union	96.0
Poland	81.7
China	73.6
Hungary	65.2
France	16.5
Italy	14.0
West Germany	10.7
United Kingdom	10.7
United States	1.3

Source: Adapted from Stanley Fischer, "Privatization in East European Transformation," in Christopher Clague and Gordon C. Rausser, eds., *The Emergence of Market Economies in Eastern Europe* (Oxford: Basil Blackwell, 1992), 230.

Note: State sector percentages are measured by value added.

But, moving on, I don't think you comprehend the enormity of the challenge that privatization presents. [*Flipping to another chart*] Examine Chart 7, and you will see that in the centrally planned economies, the state controls from 65 to 97 percent of the economy. There are some 2,300 state enterprises in Hungary; 7,500 in Poland; and 26,000 in Yugoslavia.[13] And as daunting as these numbers are, they pale in comparison to the republics of the former Soviet Union, where there are as many as 46,000 state-owned industrial firms, and another 760,000 state-owned trade enter-

---

[13] Alan H. Gelb and Cheryl W. Gray, *The Transformation of Economies in Central and Eastern Europe* (Washington, D.C.: World Bank, 1991), 39.

prises.[14] To put these numbers into further perspective, I must remind you that the total number of all state enterprises privatized in all countries around the entire world since 1980 stands at 6,800.[15] Indeed, Britain's much-touted privatization program of the 1980s shifted only two dozen firms from state control, representing a mere 4.5 percent of GNP.[16] At that pace, it would take a millennium for us to privatize!

ADVISOR: Not necessarily. We must distinguished between two parallel routes to privatization. The first is privatization "from above," by which enterprises operated by the state are transferred to private ownership and control. The second is privatization "from below," by which completely new, privately owned businesses are encouraged to form.

PRIME MINISTER: Let's focus on the first route, privatization from above. Given the extraordinary degree of state control I've just sketched, how can we possibly privatize state enterprises in my lifetime or that of my children or my children's children? It's easy enough to privatize retail establishments—barber shops, corner

---

[14] S. Shatalin et al., *500 Days: Transition to the Market* (New York: St. Martin's Press, 1991), 65.

[15] World Bank, "Privatization: The Lessons of Experience" (Study by the Country Economics Department, 1992), 7.

[16] Stanley Fischer, "Privatization in East European Transformation," in Christopher Clague and Gordon C. Rausser, eds., *The Emergence of Market Economies in Eastern Europe* (Oxford: Basil Blackwell, 1992), 229; "Creating the Invisible Hand," *Economist*, May 11, 1991, 63. For an in-depth analysis of the British privatization experience, see John Vickers and George Yarrow, *Privatization: An Economic Analysis* (Cambridge, Mass.: MIT Press, 1988). For an assessment of performance by Western public enterprises, see William G. Shepherd, *Public Enterprise: Economic Analysis of Theory and Practice* (Lexington, Mass.: Lexington Books, 1976), and Richard Pryke, *Nationalized Industries: Policies and Performance since 1968* (Oxford: Robertson, 1981).

groceries, restaurants, and family-sized operations. But what do we do with the inefficient industrial dinosaurs?

ADVISOR: One quick and easy way would be simply to give them away. Assign the ownership of each enterprise to its current workforce. Give the workers ownership shares, which can be bought and sold. Then your economy will be privatized. And the initial distribution of these ownership shares doesn't really matter once a market for shares is established. Before long, controlling interests will be purchased by groups able to manage the enterprises effectively.[17]

PRIME MINISTER: You astound me. What you propose is a quick route to riots. Workers at modern, profitable enterprises would be delighted. The value of their shares would make them rich beyond their wildest dreams. But what about the workers at antiquated, obsolete, and hopelessly unprofitable enterprises? They would get nothing. And what about the rest of the population? By their sacrifices and the sweat of their brow was the people's state built. Their contributions have sustained its enterprises.[18] Their courageous protests precipitated the collapse of Communist tyranny. Do you really think they'll passively accept a hole in their pockets, while a fabulously wealthy minority luxuriates in the collectively produced clover? Never!

ADVISOR: Well, then, give *all* your citizens ownership shares in state enterprises, which they can buy or sell

---

[17] See Becker, "Why Cold-Turkey Capitalism," 10; and Jack Kemp, "Houses to the People: An Open Letter to Boris Yeltsin," *Policy Review* Winter 1992, 4.

[18] János Kornai, *The Road to a Free Economy* (New York: W. W. Norton, 1990), p. 90.

as they see fit.[19] This is another way of privatizing your economy. It has the virtue of generating widespread national support for economic transformation, because it allows everybody to share in the wealth.

PRIME MINISTER: You are a dreamer. How would we possibly handle the astronomical number of stock shares created? Each individual enterprise would have to issue tens of millions of shares of stock—a share for every citizen. Our "securities exchange" consists of a few personal computers. Where would we find the thousands of experienced stockbrokers and lawyers needed to handle the enormous volume of transactions?

ADVISOR: We'll be glad to ship you all of them you need— free of charge.

PRIME MINISTER: What about children, the aged, and the infirm? Who would be responsible for their holdings? With each enterprise owned by millions of small stockholders, how would the owners possibly be able to effectively monitor the behavior and performance of the firms' management? Given the enormous economic hardship of our people, most would immediately sell their shares for a pittance, enabling a wealthy few quickly to purchase control of our economy.[20] And what about agriculture and our huge state collective farms?

ADVISOR: Give them away too.

PRIME MINISTER: How do you divide up hillsides, for-

[19] Milton Friedman, "Using the Market for Social Development," in James A. Dorn and Wang Xi, eds., *Economic Reform in China: Problems and Prospects* (Chicago: University of Chicago Press, 1990), 13.

[20] See David Stark, "Privatization in Hungary: From Plan to Market or From Plan to Clan?" *East European Politics and Societies* 6 (Fall 1990): 386–88.

ests, and fields? Good land and bad land? How do you divide thirty tractors among three-hundred families—especially when the tractors are monstrous machines designed for cultivating vast tracts of land, not small, privately owned farms?[21]

ADVISOR: Just take a page from Adam Smith and let the invisible hand do your privatizing for you.

PRIME MINISTER: What do you mean?

ADVISOR: Spontaneous privatization—give your enterprises to whoever takes them.

PRIME MINISTER: You mean to whoever steals them?

ADVISOR: Call it what you will. As Zhvanetsky says, "Citizens steal and the country gets rich!"

PRIME MINISTER: It's theft!

ADVISOR: Superficially, it may appear to be arbitrary seizure and theft. But a more sophisticated analysis suggests it may be the most realistic, most feasible way to privatize your economy. Let's face facts: The real economic world in which we live is just as far from the romanticized version of ideal socialism as it is from that of ideal capitalism. It's a world in which everyone cheats, pads reports, exchanges goods illegally—all of which enables the economy to survive. With spontaneous privatization, enterprises will be plucked by those who most want them and who can most efficiently manage them, as if by an invisible hand.[22]

PRIME MINISTER: Oh, they'll be plucked, all right—the way a wolf plucks chickens. What you call efficiency is what Muscovites call *korruptsia* ("corruption"), and

---

[21] Padma Desai, "Reforming the Soviet Grain Economy," *American Economic Review* 82 (May 1992): 49–54.

[22] For a proposal along this line, see *Current Digest of the Soviet Press* 42, no. 49 (1990): 11.

we have had our fill of it since the regime's collapse. Others refer to it as "nomenklatura plunderization": Apparatchiks who terrorized and preyed on the people under Communism, now enrich themselves under the fledgling democratic-market regime. They steal the people's property and personally profit from it.

The police reports on state theft are stunning. Bribes are paid to facilitate the theft of goods from state enterprises, to get the guards to look the other way, to induce railroads and trucks to haul the contraband, to get customs officials to wave the cargo across the border.[23] The managers of one state research agency established a private firm, generously transferred state computers to this firm, and then turned around and sold the computers at prices a hundred times higher than what they initially paid themselves.[24] Others have implemented similar scams with oil reserves, copper and tin deposits, retail stores, hotel chains, and brokerage operations.[25] When apprehended, the malefactors say, "Ah, you just don't understand market relations." I am sure you wouldn't tolerate that in your own country.[26]

ADVISOR: You complain about all the mafias and racketeers, but there is more honest trade today than when

[23] Steve Coll and Michael Dobbs, "Rampant Corruption Fuels Capital Flight from Russia," *Washington Post* (Jan. 31, 1993): A1.

[24] Hiatt, "In Russia, Take the Ruble and Run," *Washington Post Weekly* May 25–31, 1992, 15.

[25] "Tyumen Oil, Gas Barons Resist Clampdown," *Current Digest of the Soviet Press* 44, no. 1 (1992): 25–26; "'Shady' Deals Spur New Agency in Hungary," *Bloc*, April/May 1990, 4; "The Exchange after a Time of Testing," *Current Digest of the Soviet Press* 43, no. 25 (1991): 26–27.

[26] See Louis Uchitelle, "Stealing toward Russian Capitalism," *New York Times*, Mar. 8, 1992, sec. 3, p. 1.

your country was run by the all-embracing mafia that was the Communist Party.[27] In your circumstances, I'd consider it a small price to pay for a vastly better economy. Put it on the bill as one more—but at least the final—cost of decades of Communist misrule. How much does it matter if the former elite become the new owners? Any private profit-maximizing owner is better than none. The sooner your economy's resources are managed according to rational criteria, the sooner your standard of living will begin to improve.[28] Buying off the corrupt nomenklatura may be the cheapest, quickest way to neutralize their obstruction of your economic transformation program.[29]

PRIME MINISTER: I think you have studied economic theory too much. Those most advantaged in such spontaneous privatizations are the apparatchiks, who have the best contacts and the best access to materials, equipment, and financial capital. They're the ones writing the rules for economic transition. Naturally they will provide plenty of advantages and loopholes for themselves. But that doesn't mean that they are the best economic managers and entrepreneurs. In fact, such wild privatization makes it likely that the same incompetents will continue to mismanage the economy under different guises. Worse, they will find it easier and more lucrative to make their profits by manipulating the state, rather than by genuinely enhancing the economic performance of their enterprises.

---

[27] Jeffrey Sachs, "Home Alone 2," *New Republic*, Dec. 21, 1992, 25.

[28] The case as advocated by some in favor of spontaneous privatization is reported by Stark, "Privatization in Hungary," 368.

[29] For a proposal along these lines, see Jan Winiecki, *Resistance to Change in the Soviet Economic System* (London: Routledge, 1991), chap. 4.

It seems to me that only equality of opportunity to acquire state enterprises will ensure that they will go to those fittest to manage them. To permit such nomenklatura privatization—or to actively encourage it, as you suggest—would be the quickest way to discredit the market economy in the eyes of our people, and to subvert our restructuring efforts.[30]

ADVISOR: Well, then, since you don't care for any of my giveaway privatization policies, the only alternative is to *sell* your state enterprises to private owners.

PRIME MINISTER: But there is only one problem. Who actually owns these enterprises? Who has the right to sell them?

ADVISOR: The state owns them, of course.

PRIME MINISTER: But who, exactly, is "the state"? Is it the citizens? If so, they already "own" the enterprises, and no privatization program is necessary. To say they belong to everyone is to say they belong to no one. Consider the dilemma of the Soviet Union: in theory, the Soviet government owns the enterprises, but the Soviet government no longer exists. Do the republics now own the enterprises? Do local governments own them? local communities? management and workers?

ADVISOR: For purposes of our conversation, let's assume someone or something owns them.

PRIME MINISTER: You economists are in love with assumptions!

ADVISOR: That may be, but let's proceed. Now, to priva-

---

[30] For general analyses of the problem, see Simon Johnson and Heidi Kroll, "Managerial Strategies for Spontaneous Privatization," *Soviet Economy,* 1991, 281–321; and Anthony Levitas and Piotr Strzalkowski, "What Does 'Propertisation of the Nomenklatura' Really Mean?" *Communist Economies* 2 (1990): 413–16.

tize these state enterprises you simply sell them off—
put them up for auction to the highest bidder.

PRIME MINISTER: A marvelous proposition. But how do
you sell property that belongs to nobody, and has no
value, to people who have no money? You take a lot for
granted. For example, don't we need a stock market in
order to determine the value of these enterprises?

ADVISOR: Yes, that is why you must immediately establish one.

PRIME MINISTER: Wouldn't the value of the state enterprises being privatized depend upon their competitive
status? In other words, if they were privatized as monopolies, wouldn't their future profits, and hence their
present market value, be much greater than if they
were restructured and sold as competitive plants and
operations?

ADVISOR: Yes, but you must avoid the short-run temptation of trying to obtain greater government revenues by
privatizing state enterprises as monopolies. The British
privatization program failed badly in this regard: short-
term political advantage was won, but longer-lived
gains from competition were sacrificed.[31]

PRIME MINISTER: There is a further problem. The book
value of our state enterprises far exceeds the savings of
our people available to purchase them. One conservative estimate puts the combined value of these assets
at three times the per capita gross income of our citizens. If our total national savings were used solely to
purchase state enterprises, and if all the people's dis-

[31] See Richard E. Caves, "Lessons from Privatization in Britain," *Journal
of Economic Behavior and Organization* 13 (1990): 156–69; and John Vickers
and George Yarrow, *Privatization: An Economic Analysis* (Cambridge, Mass.:
MIT Press, 1989), 426–28.

posable incomes were also drawn on, it would still take four years to privatize merely half of the state sector.[32] To compound the problem, our economy is little more than an open-air museum of ancient industrial technology.[33] In fact, at one of our textile plants, the only profit last year reportedly came from the sale of a spinning machine—a 1911 model purchased by a museum in Munich![34]

ADVISOR: Don't try to outguess the market. Ignore the value of the enterprises carried on the accounting books. It is irrelevant. The market will decide the value of these enterprises. The top bid is the only relevant economic value.

PRIME MINISTER: And once again the advantage would go to the already rich and powerful—who are the only ones who can afford to pay. The people will find the meat gone and only the bones left. The result will be a tremendous concentration of economic control in the hands of the few with the financial wherewithal to bid.

ADVISOR: You chide me for making assumptions. But you always assume the worst.

PRIME MINISTER: I make no assumption. This is precisely what happened when Chile privatized its enterprises during the 1970s under the leadership of the "Chicago Boys." Control of the economy quickly passed into the hands of some twenty giant conglomerate/

---

[32] Shatalin et al., *500Days*, 66–67; Igor V. Filatotchev, "Privatisation in the USSR: Economic and Social Problems," *Communist Economies* 3 (1991): 485.

[33] V. A. Naishul, "Problems of Creating a Market in the USSR," *Communist Economies* 2 (1990): 284.

[34] Reported in Amos Elon, "In a Former Country," *New York Review of Books*, Apr. 23, 1992, 37.

financial groups. Within five years, over half the assets of the country's largest two hundred firms were controlled by just two of these groups. The subsequent collapse of these megaholding companies required a massive renationalization and bailout program by the government. Cynics refer to it as the "Chicago road to socialism"![35]

ADVISOR: You don't have to limit the buying to domestic bidders alone. Foreign sources of capital would be readily available to join in the auctioning process. Their participation would help prevent the consolidation of control that concerns you.[36]

PRIME MINISTER: Sell our patrimony to foreigners for a song? Our people would never stand for such humiliation.

ADVISOR: Explain to them how we all must live in a global economy these days.

PRIME MINISTER: So that they'll smash Toyotas with sledgehammers?

ADVISOR: Very well, then, consider a combination of my foregoing proposals. You first create stock shares for the state enterprises. Then you allocate a portion of these shares to the workers and management of each

[35] See Pan A. Yotopoulos, "The (Rip)Tide of Privatization: Lessons from Chile," World Development, 1989, 683–702; Sebastian Edwards and Alejandra Cox Edwards, Monetarism and Liberalization: The Chilean Experiment (Cambridge, Mass.: Ballinger Publishing Co., 1987); and Antonio Schneider, "Supply-Side Economics in a Small Economy: The Chilean Case," in Edward Nell, ed., Free Market Conservatism: A Critique of Theory and Practice (London: Allen and Unwin, 1984), 226. For an extensive survey of the privatization challenge generally, see Morris Bornstein, "Privatization in Eastern Europe," Communist Economies 4 (1992): 283–320.

[36] Merton J. Peck and Thomas J. Richardson, eds., What Is To Be Done? Proposals for the Soviet Transition to the Market (New Haven: Yale University Press, 1991), 35.

enterprise in order to give them an incentive to work productively and efficiently. You also allocate a portion of the shares to the public at large, enabling them to participate in the privatization program. To ensure that the managements of the enterprises behave in the best interests of the new private owners, you assign additional portions of the stock to financial holding companies, which you can trust to exercise vigilant oversight. And in order to prevent concentration of financial control, you can create as many of these holding companies as you like.[37]

The permutations and combinations of specific features of privatization programs are unlimited. The Polish privatization plan, for example, is based primarily on free distribution of vouchers for ownership shares to the citizenry, with the stipulation that these vouchers must be invested in any of a multitude of mutual funds created and managed by expert analysts. The Hungarians, on the other hand, are avoiding vouchers altogether; they are relying on sales of ownership shares in their firms to those investors—foreign or domestic—willing to pay the highest price. Meanwhile, Czechoslovakia is implementing perhaps the most economically sophisticated privatization scheme: vouchers are being distributed that entitle citizens to bid "points" for shares; auctions will proceed, share prices will be adjusted, and rebidding will take place until an equilibrium, market-clearing price is reached.[38]

---

[37] See David Lipton and Jeffrey Sachs, "Privatization in Eastern Europe: The Case of Poland," in Vittorio Corbo, Fabrizio Coricelli, and Jan Bossak, eds., *Reforming Central and Eastern European Economies* (Washington, D.C.: World Bank, 1991), 293–334; and Oliver Blanchard et. al., *Reform in Eastern Europe* (Cambridge, Mass.: MIT Press, 1991), xiii.

[38] See "Creating the Invisible Hand," *Economist,* May 11, 1991, 63–66;

PRIME MINISTER: We used to say that religion comforts the masses by assuring them that there is life after death. After conversing with our economic advisors, I am comforted by the thought that there is death after life.

ADVISOR: Take comfort in this: the fact of the matter is that it makes little difference who the initial owners are. Once private property rights are assigned, resources eventually will find their way into the most efficient and productive hands, and your economy will ultimately begin to improve.[39]

PRIME MINISTER: How can you be so sure?

ADVISOR: The Coase theorem guarantees it.[40]

PRIME MINISTER: The Coase theorem guarantees revolution in the streets! Let's move on and discuss the second path of privatization you mentioned earlier, privatization from below.

ADVISOR: An excellent idea. All of our discussion thus far has addressed problems of privatization from above, that is, the task of converting state enterprises to private ownership. Privatization from below, on the other hand, is much easier. You simply encourage your people to form new, privately owned firms, which have absolutely no connection with the state. You establish a legal and political environment that enables private entrepreneurs to form new businesses from scratch, and to operate them using their own resources. Privatization from below should appeal to you.

"Going for Broke," ibid., May 16, 1992, 85–86; and Peter Passell, "A Capitalist Free-for-All in Czechoslovakia," *New York Times*, Apr. 12, 1992, sec. 3, p. 10.

[39] Roberts and LaFollette, *Meltdown*, 113.

[40] Ronald H. Coase, "The Problem of Social Cost," *Journal of Law and Economics* 3 (Oct. 1960): 1.

PRIME MINISTER: Why is that?

ADVISOR: Because it's so simple. All that's required is for your government to get out of the way. Dismantle the bureaucratic barriers that obstruct private enterprise, abolish the misguided measures you enacted in the past to suppress the private sector, and private firms will sprout like mushrooms.

PRIME MINISTER: Utopians always concentrate on the big issues and conveniently ignore the critical details. Suppose we were to implement your spontaneous privatization policy, for example. In Russia, the forces of corruption and monopoly are already flocking around the state committee charged with the disposal of buildings and land.[41] Given their political influence, powerful apparatchiks will establish themselves as capitalists and will not only obtain control of state enterprises but also retain political control over key materials and sources of credit. It's not farfetched to suspect that they will refuse to make those resources available to independent entrepreneurs, who may compete with them and erode their profitability. If they have the clout to steal state firms, won't they also use their clout to crush potential new competition? Similarly, the financial holding companies you propose to oversee newly privatized state enterprises, and to own sizable ownership stakes in them, may refuse to lend funds to new firms, which might compete with their clients and reduce the value of their stock holdings. Hostile government officials also harass potential entrepreneurs because they consider them a threat to

---

[41] Maggie Mahar, "Wolf at the Door: A Failing Economy Threatens Survival of the New Russia," *Barron's*, Oct. 19, 1992, 20.

their authority and power. They often wage war against newcomers by denying them licenses, arbitrarily raising their taxes, impeding their access to office space, and demanding bribes and payoffs.[42]

Moreover, given the Communist infatuation with "gigantomania" and vertical integration, how will independent private entrepreneurs obtain access to vital inputs? And if they can't obtain such access, how can they hope to establish themselves "from below" as viable entities?

ADVISOR: I think you underestimate the ingenuity of your people. Decades of rationing, shortages, bartering, and black markets under communism may have rendered them far more resourceful than you imagine. Already, hundreds of thousands of new private firms are sprouting up in the wake of the implementation of economic liberalization in Czechoslovakia and Hungary. In Poland, for example, more than 500,000 individual proprietorships have sprung up since 1989, along with an increase of 34,000 private commercial companies (including partnerships, limited liability companies, and joint-stock firms) and an increase of some 6,000 firms in industry. All told, the private sector share of the Polish economy has soared from 19 percent in 1989 to 45 percent today. By the end of 1991, Czechoslovakia had some 5,000 incorporated firms, Hungary had 30,000, and Poland had 40,000.[43] In agriculture, the number of

[42] Joseph S. Berliner, "Restructuring the Soviet Planned Economy," in William S. Kern, ed. *From Socialism to Market Economy* (Kalamazoo, Mich.: Upjohn Institute, 1992),

[43] See Jeffrey D. Sachs, "Privatization in Russia: Some Lessons from Eastern Europe," *American Economic Review* 82 (May 1992): 44; "Pioneers of Capitalism," *Economist*, Apr. 4, 1992, 79; and Ryszard Rapacki and

private farms in Russia has skyrocketed sixfold, from 20,000 to 120,000 during the past years alone.[44] Perhaps you should have more faith in the magic of the market.

PRIME MINISTER: The Poles say that pessimism is informed optimism. Even if privatizing our economy were the only task we faced, it would present a monumental challenge. But, of course, it's not the only problem. In fact, I am beginning to wonder if it's really possible to achieve privatization in the midst of hyperinflation, hyperunemployment, hyperdeficits—and hyperchaos.

ADVISOR: Economics teaches us that life is a stream of choices, not all of them pleasant. So look on the bright side: the alternative of not privatizing is far worse.

PRIME MINISTER: On that cheerful note, let's call it a day!

Susan J. Linz, "Privatization in Transition Economies" (Econometrics and Economic Theory Paper 9011, Michigan State University, Mar. 1992), 15.

[44] Serge Schmemann, "Free Market Ideas Grow on Russian Farms," *New York Times*, Oct. 6, 1992, 1.

DAY 5 — STABILIZATION

Stabilization turns out to be a seamless web. The conferees discuss fiscal policy, monetary policy, and the Big Bang model.

PRIME MINISTER: As you pointed out during our initial meeting, a reasonable macro equilibrium is a fundamental requirement if a market economy is to operate effectively. We have to bring aggregate demand into balance with aggregate supply in order to achieve stability in the general price level. Only then can the market be an effective instrument for a rational allocation of resources and a mechanism for determining relative prices.

ADVISOR: You're absolutely right. Moving to a market economy requires a sharp shift in the instruments of economic control. You must move away from detailed, intricate microeconomic controls, and to broad macroeconomic controls. In centrally planned economies, as you well know, stabilization policy involves micro control of individual prices, individual wages, and individual production decisions. In a market economy, these controls are replaced by macro monetary and fiscal policies. Instead of restricting credit to particular firms, you control the aggregate supply of credit available to the economy at large. This shift requires relaxing controls on the micro variables, while imposing strict controls on the macro variables.[1]

[1] William D. Nordhaus, "Stabilizing the Soviet Economy," in Merton J.

PRIME MINISTER: How should we go about implementing such macroeconomic stabilization policy?

ADVISOR: There is no mystery about the principles of macroeconomics. Insufficient aggregate demand means unemployment, idle capacity, and lost production. Excessive aggregate demand means inflation—general increases in prices and money incomes, bringing forth little or no gains in output and real income. The objective of stabilization policies is to minimize these deviations—in other words, to keep overall demand in step with the full employment production potential of the economy.

PRIME MINISTER: That calls for a sound fiscal policy.

ADVISOR: Yes. Government expenditures and taxes affect total employment and production by influencing the total volume of spending for goods and services. Direct government purchases are themselves part of the aggregate demand for national output. So are so-called transfer payments, such as social security, unemployment insurance benefits, veterans' compensation, government employees' pension benefits, and so on. Both government purchases and transfer payments add to private incomes, thereby stimulating consumption and investment. The taxes imposed by government have the opposite effect: they reduce personal and business incomes, thereby putting a damper on private spending.

The relationship between government expenditures and the amount of taxes collected determines govern-

Peck and Thomas J. Richardson, eds., *What Is to Be Done? Proposals for the Soviet Transition to the Market* (New Haven: Yale University Press, 1991), '04–5.

ment's net fiscal impact on the economy. If expenditures exceed taxes, then the government budget is in deficit, which has an expansionary impact on the economy. If taxes exceed expenditures, then the government budget is in surplus, which has a contractionary impact on the economy.

PRIME MINISTER: Taxes and tax policy present an immediate problem, however. Traditionally the bulk of our taxes, in some cases as much as 90 percent, have been collected by our state ministries, which have simply appropriated the "profits" generated by state enterprises.[2] So, you see, we didn't need a corporate income tax. Nor did we need a personal income tax; the government set wages and salaries low enough so that, in effect, it collected a tax on incomes at the source. Nor did we need a sales tax; the government set prices of "luxuries," such as liquor, tobacco, and automobiles, at arbitrarily high levels in order to swell the cash coffers of government. It is not surprising, therefore, that today we don't have a tax system as you know it. Nor do we have an expert collection agency capable of functioning as does your Internal Revenue Service.

Moreover, once we abandon price and wage controls, and once we begin privatizing the state enterprises that the government used as "cash cows," the problem of collecting revenues will become a nightmare. Unwittingly and perversely, the very process of reform will become an instrument for undermining effective macro stabilization.[3]

---

[2] OECD, *Reforming the Economies of Central and Eastern Europe* (Paris: OECD, 1992), 33.

[3] Ronald I. McKinnon, "Taxation, Money, and Credit in a Liberalizing

ADVISOR: It's all the more urgent that you compensate for this loss of government tax receipts. You must put in place new taxes—income taxes, excise taxes, and perhaps a value-added tax—and create a professional tax administration machinery to collect them.

PRIME MINISTER: That's reasonable, but not so easy to do. As privatization spreads, it will become easier to evade all forms of taxation. Under communism, our people learned one lesson well, perhaps too well: evade and obstruct government laws, rules, and regulations wherever and whenever possible. Now we seem to be caught in a fiscal trap: the larger the private sector becomes, the harder it becomes to collect taxes and to balance the budget.

ADVISOR: Sure it's difficult. You also must proceed with extreme prudence. Excessive taxes, or excessive enforcement of tax laws, will encourage even more tax evasion—or, worse, will discourage your people from engaging in private enterprise altogether.[4]

PRIME MINISTER: What about monetary policy?

ADVISOR: Monetary policy is the second major instrument that government can use to achieve macroeconomic stabilization. Interpreted in its broadest sense, monetary policy encompasses all government actions affecting the liquidity of the economy and the availability and cost of credit. By injecting additional credit into the economy, the central bank implements a stim-

---

Socialist Economy," in Christopher Clague and Gordon C. Rausser, eds., *The Emergence of Market Economies in Eastern Europe* (Cambridge, Mass.: Blackwell, 1992), 109ff.

[4] János Kornai, "The Postsocialist Transition and the State: Reflections in the Light of Hungarian Fiscal Problems," *American Economic Review* 82 (May 1992): 11–14.

ulative monetary policy. Conversely, by withdrawing credit from the economy, the central bank implements a contractionary monetary policy.

PRIME MINISTER: Here again, however, reality is more complex than textbook abstractions. In our centrally planned economy, the monetary and credit system traditionally has played a negligible role—a passive role. Basically, its purpose was bookkeeping. Our central planners directly determined the allocation of physical resources and inputs, as well as the physical production of goods and materials. They would say, "We need so many tons of heat-treated aluminum plate to make so many MIG-29s. Or, we need so many tons of steel I-beams for the construction of bridges." Interest rates, borrowing, and lending were largely irrelevant. Cash balances were essentially an afterthought, mechanically adjusted to match physical production plans determined in advance.[5] As a result, our financial markets, and our ability to use financial instruments are woefully undeveloped.

ADVISOR: Rest assured that privatization and the unrelenting press of financial survival will dramatically enhance your country's financial capabilities.

PRIME MINISTER: As a well-known Russian saying has it, life is not as simple as it appears at first glance. But the transition to privatization severely compounds the difficulty of implementing the kind of monetary policy you describe. Our enterprises are circumventing monetary controls, and in effect "manufacturing" their own money supply, through a process of interfirm credit—what is now referred to as involuntary credit

[5] McKinnon, "Taxation, Money, and Credit," 112.

or pseudocredit. Firms purchase materials from other firms on credit, and then simply refuse to pay their bills. They ship products at ridiculously inflated prices, which they know full well their buyers will never pay; they then enter the amounts in their account books as credits and record an inflated, fictitious paper profit. This phony credit has exploded. In Russia, for example, pseudocredit in 1992 jumped from 39 billion rubles to 3.1 trillion rubles, accounting for as much as 40 percent of total enterprise credit; by August 1992, nearly half of all the output of Russian enterprises was being delivered to buyers without payment—and without any hope of receiving payment.[6] Because so many firms are playing this game, few of them are willing to press for payment, since doing so would snowball into financial collapse for all of them.[7] It also compounds the difficulty of defining what constitutes "money supply" and controlling it effectively.

ADVISOR: Again, privatization, market forces, financial discipline, and a new legal system will solve the problem. Allowing ten major bankruptcies should make the point. Once firms and banks understand that the state will not stand ready to bail them out—once they confront genuinely "hard budget constraints"—they either will cease granting credit that they have no prospect of collecting, or they will fail. The key is to create a strong central monetary authority, able to withstand political pressure for undisciplined credit creation.

PRIME MINISTER: Yet another conundrum arises, how-

---

[6] *Current Digest of the Post-Soviet Press*, Sept. 2, 1992, 2; Louis Uchitelle, "Finger Pointing on Russian Debt," *New York Times*, July 28, 1992, C2.

[7] Blue Ribbon Commission, *Hungary in Transformation* (Indianapolis: Hudson Institute, 1990), 48–54.

ever, because a tight monetary policy raises the cost of credit, making it even more difficult for new private firms to establish themselves.[8]

ADVISOR: It's my turn now to cite one of your Russian proverbs: In the absence of luck, even misfortune can help.

PRIME MINISTER: Perhaps. Which is more effective, monetary or fiscal policy?

ADVISOR: I'm afraid macroeconomists are sharply divided on this question. Monetarists contend that monetary policy is the most important instrument for promoting macroeconomic growth and stability: They dismiss fiscal policy as fraught with flaws and deficiencies. Fiscalists, on the other hand, insist that fiscal policy is indispensable for fostering macroeconomic stabilization; they chide the monetarists for simplistically advocating that "money is all that matters." Rational expectationists reject all macroeconomic policy —monetary and fiscal alike—as futile, because they believe that rational economic agents (a category that includes everyone, according to these theorists) anticipate any government macropolicy and on the basis of that anticipation, act to further their own interests in ways that neutralize the policy in question.

PRIME MINISTER: Your response reminds me of a remark by one of your presidents, Harry S. Truman, back in the 1940s. Frustrated by economists framing their advice with "on the one hand" and "on the other hand," he expressed longing for a "one-armed" economist.

ADVISOR: A reasonable answer to your question would be

---

[8] Zbigniew M. Fallenbuchl, "Polish Privatization Policy," *Comparative Economic Studies* 33 (Summer 1991): 61.

that both monetary and fiscal policy are essential. Neither can stabilize the economy by itself. They have to be used in tandem. When the economy is in the midst of recession, government must pursue a mix of policies: increasing expenditures, cutting taxes, easing credit, and pumping money into circulation. When the economy is overheated—when too much money is chasing too few goods—it must do the opposite. In other words, a macro stabilization policy must apply the throttle or the brake to the economic engine as the situation may require. The trick is not to overdo it in either direction.

PRIME MINISTER: That is the theory. But the situation in which we find ourselves now, during this crucial transition period, is inflation and the danger of hyperinflation. For us, this is a novel phenomenon.

ADVISOR: I disagree. Under communism, you experienced what we call repressed inflation. Consumers suffered from pervasive shortages and spent long hours queuing up for the scarce goods that were available. Yet the government did not permit prices to rise, a move that would have both "rationed" the available supply and acted as a stimulant to producers to increase that supply. In other words, it did not permit prices to bring demand and supply into balance. As a result consumers accumulated forced savings—hoards of money that was not spent or was unspendable. This monetary overhang was an indirect measure of the inflation that bedeviled the system, but it was hidden from view by the rigid price controls imposed by the government.

PRIME MINISTER: This repressed inflation has now become overt inflation. With the abandonment of price controls, we no longer have the erstwhile bureaucratic brakes and barriers to constrain the buildup of excess aggregate demand. With the freeing of wages, we have lost our ability to prevent an increase in household incomes from fueling the pressure on the price level. And the temptation of the government to increase the money supply to ameliorate these problems further compounds them. Particularly nettlesome is the government's proclivity to incur budget deficits and to have the central bank finance these deficits by issuing more money.

ADVISOR: That is precisely why you have to implement a stern stabilization policy and why you have to do so promptly.[9]

PRIME MINISTER: I am afraid you don't appreciate the enormity of the problem. Given our current circumstances, a strict austerity policy would not liberate us, but strangle us. Inflation has been exceeding expectations in almost all countries in the region, irrespective of whether the free market reform process began only recently or has been under way for some time. In Poland, while the inflation rate is nowhere near the 2,000 percent it hit in 1989, it was still running at 60 percent in 1991. In Hungary the rate is 35 percent; in Czechoslovakia, 54 percent; in Russia, possibly as high as 2,500 percent (with interest rates of 84 percent). At the same time, industrial output has fallen precipitously—anywhere from 10 to 50 percent, and in some cases by twice the amount your country experienced during the Great Depression. Unemployment is at lev-

[9] David Lipton and Jeffrey Sachs, "Creating a Market Economy in Eastern Europe: The Case of Poland," *Brookings Papers on Economic Activity* 1 (1990): 89.

els not previously seen in the postwar era. Moreover, it may well rise in the short and medium term, as managers come under pressure to shed nonessential labor and to increase the productivity of their enterprises in order to meet the standards of the world market.[10]

ADVISOR: While there's no question that people are suffering, the statistics you cite exaggerate the severity of the economic pain. For example, official statistics do not capture the explosive growth of the private sector. Nor do they convey the welfare gains due to the higher quality of goods now being produced, or the greater variety of goods from which consumers can now choose. Also, some of your efficiency gains paradoxically can show up in ways that suggest that economic affairs are getting worse rather than better. More rational organization of production, for example, reduces wasteful cross-hauling between factories, which, in turn, results in a decline in estimates of GDP in the transportation sector.[11]

PRIME MINISTER: Nevertheless, we find ourselves in a situation where we are forced to deal with simultaneous inflation and recession—what your economists call stagflation. How can a macro stabilization policy deal with this problem? Is it not advisable to reinforce

[10] U.S. Central Intelligence Agency, Directorate of Intelligence, "Eastern Europe: Struggling to Stay on the Reform Track" (July 1992); OECD, *Reforming the Economies*, 23–25; Steven Erlanger, "Newest 'Reforms' Will Vex Russians," *New York Times*, July 1, 1992, A5; A. Kregel and Egon Matzner, "Agenda for the Reconstruction of Central and Eastern Europe," *Challenge*, Sept./Oct. 1992, 33–40.

[11] Andrew Berg and Jeffrey Sachs, "Structural Adjustment and International Trade in Eastern Europe: The Case of Poland," *Economic Policy*, Apr. 1992, 119, 142, 148–49.

monetary and fiscal policy with an "incomes" policy to control wage and price inflation directly?

ADVISOR: As I already told you, I am firmly opposed to an incomes policy that entails price and wage controls. I do see some justification for wage controls until the monetary overhang, created by repressed inflation, is eliminated. In general, however, I think there is no alternative to eliminating the budget deficits, which in most of the countries in this region approach 20 percent of GNP, and to stop printing the money that is financing the deficits.

PRIME MINISTER: That is a commendable austerity program. But I can't help reacting to it, as my Italian friends would, by asking: From what pulpit comes this sermon? Need I remind you that as of 1992 the U.S. government was spending more than four dollars for every 3 dollars it collected in revenue: In fact, it hemorrhaged red ink at a record pace that year—about $1 billion a day, or $11,574 a second—and by late summer its debt had surpassed $4 trillion.[12]

ADVISOR: That is certainly true, but I wouldn't suggest that you emulate our record of nonfeasance and misfeasance on this score. In the past we rationalized our national debt by saying that "we owe it to ourselves," but the debt has now grown to such size that many economists contend that it undermines U.S. prosperity.

PRIME MINISTER: Your recommendation is sound—in theory. But let me spell out some practical implica-

---

[12] For a perspective on the U.S. debt, see Robert L. Heilbroner and Peter Bernstein, *The Debt and the Deficit: False Alarms/Real Possibilities* (New York: W. W. Norton, 1989), and Robert Eisner, *How Real Is the Federal Deficit?* (New York: Free Press, 1986).

tions. The Cold War is over. It makes sense, therefore, to cut the armed forces of the old Warsaw Pact nations by several million men. But where are these people to go? What are they to do? We have neither housing nor jobs for them. They would become part of a growing army of the unemployed. What about the manufacturing firms that once were the backbone of the military-industrial complex? They can't convert to civilian production overnight. Should the government keep them alive with massive subsidies—with predictable consequences for the budget deficit? What about the giant enterprises—those decrepit dinosaurs in the state sector—which can't survive in a competitive world without government aid? Should the government bail them out? For how long? At what cost? When an economy is in a free-fall spiral into depression—with plummeting production, burgeoning unemployment, collapsing living standards—that is certainly not the time to worry about balancing the budget.[13]

ADVISOR: I won't pretend that shock therapy is a pleasant experience, but it is imperative if the patient is to be restored to health.

PRIME MINISTER: I am astounded by your lack of empathy for our problems. Perhaps a parallel to your own situation in the United States will clarify my argument. When the Cold War came to a sudden and unanticipated end, Americans believed that defense expenditures would be cut drastically—that they would be entitled to a "peace dividend." Did that happen? Did

---

[13] Mortimer B. Zuckerman, "Rethinking Aid to Russia," *U.S. News & World Report*, Sept. 21, 1992, 90. See also Nikolai Petrakov, "Myths and Reefs," *Moscow News Weekly*, July 12–19, 1992, 8.

Grumman Aircraft suddenly start building high-speed trains instead of F-16s for the Navy? Did Electric Boat discontinue construction of the Seawolf nuclear submarine (at a cost of two billion dollars apiece) and start building pleasure craft? No, and the government didn't force them to do so. Why? Because it would have caused massive unemployment, which could not be absorbed in a depression-ridden economy. Instead, your country expanded its exports of jet fighters to Taiwan and Saudi Arabia.

In theory, we know that many of our defense plants should be closed or converted to civilian production. In theory, we know that inefficient state enterprises—Poland's Nowa Huta steel mill, Russia's Uralmash heavy machinery giant, and a good many others—ought to be condemned to bankruptcy. In theory, we know that this is supposed to liberate their employees to go into more productive employment elsewhere in the economy, thus raising the economy's overall efficiency and productivity. But as a practical matter, we know that the private sector is nowhere near ready to absorb the surge of displaced workers. [*Flipping backwards to Chart 2*] Let's look at the unemployment projections again. In Poland, by 1994, unemployment may reach 20 percent of the labor force: in the former Soviet Union, where every fifth person is working in a state defense plant or serving in the military, it may reach 24 percent. So you must forgive us, if we temper theory with pragmatism. In theory we want inefficient, redundant firms to go bankrupt, but not in practice—not yet anyway.

ADVISOR: I am more empathetic than you think. I recognize that you have serious problems. The intractable budget deficit is certainly one of them. But do you know what I think is the biggest problem? Pessimism—the inability to accept good news; the perception that the glass is always half-empty, never half-full. And none of your leaders has come forward to proclaim, "There is nothing to fear but fear itself," as did one of our presidents, Franklin D. Roosevelt, during the Depression—instead, there is no shortage of those who constantly warn, "We have everything to fear."[14]

PRIME MINISTER: Why are you surprised? Having just thrown off decades of Marxist ideology, we are understandably wary of any and all grand utopian blueprints, cults, dogmas, and propaganda. Events have taught us to be skeptical about buying into any ideology before it proves itself in our everyday experience.

ADVISOR: Transitions have always been difficult. And they've been most difficult in the early stages. Think of Japan and the grim situation it confronted in 1947. Think of Germany and the desperate straits in which it found itself at the end of World War II. Both embraced free market economics and produced a *Wirtschaftswunder*! So did Spain, where it took twenty years to achieve success and where, in the early stages, unemployment rates of 18 to 20 percent were not uncommon.

PRIME MINISTER: Your recollection of history is quite selective. You mention Spain. As Professor Alice Amsden, an OECD advisor has pointed out, Spain had a comprehensive industrial policy, considerable support from the European Community, extensive planning and government intervention, and targeted protection

---

[14] Jeffrey Sachs, quoted in Lawrence Weschler, "Reporter at Large: Poland," *The New Yorker*, May 11, 1992, 69.

of key industries. Its reintegration into Europe was part of a deliberate regional policy. It never adopted a Big Bang approach. It was never subjected to anything like the free market, pie-in-the-sky-privatization, emphasis-on-austerity program that the IMF has been trying to foist on the ex-Communist nations of our region.[15]

The past century of capitalist experience shows that late entrants into the capitalist world market, such as Germany in the late nineteenth century, Japan in the twentieth century, and the "Young Tigers" (South Korea, Taiwan, and Singapore) in the post–World War II period, succeeded against initially superior competitors only by means of a heavily state-guided economy. It is not the wisdom of the free market that enabled these nations to grow so rapidly. They combined freedom for entrepreneurial initiative, private property, and market prices with carefully crafted industrial policies and tightly controlled foreign trade and investment. They utilized import tariffs, export incentives, tax relief, and other mechanisms to guide the development of their domestic economies. State guidance in conjunction with private enterprise explains their success.[16]

ADVISOR: I think I understand the dilemma you confront—the tremendous pressures impinging on the reform process from all sides. On the one hand, you have to deal with the strictures of the IMF in order to be eligible for the stabilization fund to finance the tran-

---

[15] Ibid., 72. See also Alice Amsden, "An Asian Plan for Eastern Europe," *New York Times*, Apr. 6, 1990.

[16] David M. Kotz, "The Direction of Soviet Economic Reform" (Working Paper no. 1992–2, Economics Department, University of Massachusetts, 1992); and Garry Jacobs, "Lessons of the Economic Transition in Russia," *Moscow News Weekly*, Aug. 16–23, 1992, 10.

sition to a market economy: Deregulate prices of goods and services! Stop subsidizing the cost of food, housing, heating, electricity! Eliminate low-interest loans to nonviable state enterprises! Don't bail out the inefficient, redundant, noncompetitive firms! Cut back expenditures on health services, pensions, and other social programs! Stop printing money and recklessly expanding bank credit! Privatize the production of goods and services! Above all, do these things all at the same time!

On the other hand, you have the pressure from the public, complaining about such astronomical price increases that virtually nobody can buy the goods now available in the shops. Pressure from overstaffed, inefficient state firms, which cannot survive without government help and which have to lay off thousands of workers if they are to become competitive in free markets. Pressure from the retirees protesting against inadequate pensions and the unemployed protesting cutbacks in benefits. Pressure from workers, who are organizing protest strikes to demonstrate the failure of wages to keep pace with the cost of living. A general malaise among the population, which sees a handful of people—those it calls speculators, mafiosi, the old nomenklatura—getting rich while the standard of living for the vast majority keeps declining. There is pervasive fear and anxiety about the future. All this is true. But if you don't face up to the challenge—if you simply print great quantities of money to paper over the burgeoning budget deficit—your reforms will fail. You won't be able to translate your dreams of a market economy into reality.

PRIME MINISTER: Yet facts are stubborn and cannot be

ignored. Even under supposedly ideal circumstances, the transition to a market economy is difficult, painful, and costly. Look at the former East Germany. Once it was unified with the Federal Republic it inherited a readymade legal, political, and economic institutional framework to ease the transition. It gained immediate access to managerial expertise capable of running a market system. Despite these advantages, the restructuring of East Germany has resulted in 40 percent of its workforce losing their jobs, a 50 percent plunge in GDP, and the need for an annual subsidy from the Berlin government of one hundred billion dollars for the indefinite future.[17]

Throughout the region the situation is foreboding: Privatization is proceeding at a snail's pace, far slower than original expectations. Inflation persists. So does unemployment. The region is in the midst of a steep and unrelenting recession. There is political gridlock. The patience of the people is wearing thin. Under the circumstances, virtually all the governments in the region have felt compelled to moderate their plans for reform and to slow down the pace of the transition.

In Poland, to cite just one example, the Mazowiecki government, which had religiously professed its commitment to a balanced budget, when confronted with political pressure, decided six months after its program had been launched to increase social expenditures at the cost of tolerating a deficit. Some leaders, in fact,

---

[17] Rudiger Dornbusch and Holger Wolf, "Economic Transition in Eastern Germany," *Brookings Papers on Economic Activity* 1 (1992): 236–41; *New York Times*, Sept. 10, 1992, A3. The Economic Commission for Europe projects the same grim prospect for the region as a whole (*Economic Bulletin for Europe*, vol. 43, Nov. 1991).

have begun to question whether it was prudent to implement a Big Bang approach in the first place— whether it would not have been wiser to introduce reforms gradually, in other words, to sequence the moves to a market economy. The same rumblings are heard in Russia today.

ADVISOR: Socialist economies have so many problems, and the problems are so interconnected, that reformers —understandably—are unsure where to begin. Where should they start? With the budget? With privatization? With property reforms? With capital markets? With reduction of subsidies? With a convertible currency? It seems to me that the case for a rapid and comprehensive transition process is overwhelming.[18] East European history has taught us the profound shortcomings of a piecemeal approach, and economic logic suggests the necessity of a rapid transition. Moreover, the macroeconomic situation in many countries is deplorable and deteriorating, and therefore requires urgent attention.

Like it or not, the transition process is a seamless web. Structural reforms cannot work without a working price system; a working price system cannot be put in place without ending excess demand and creating a convertible currency; and a credit squeeze and tight macroeconomic policy cannot be sustained unless prices are realistic so that there is a rational basis for deciding which firms should be allowed to close. At the same time, for real structural adjustment to take place under the pressures of tight demand, the macroeconomic shock must be accompanied by other measures, including selling off state assets, freeing up the private

[18] Nordhaus, "Stabilizing," 84–85.

sector, establishing procedures for bankruptcy, preparing a social safety net, and undertaking tax reform. Clearly, the reform process must be comprehensive.[19]

PRIME MINISTER: Your economic logic is flawless, but you underestimate the political aspects of the reform process. It's easy to put out a fire with someone else's hands. It's easy for an economist to recommend deregulation of prices, even though the economy is pervasively monopolized, and then leave it to government to contain the inflationary pressures such a policy generates and deal with the volatile changes in income distribution it entails. It's easy for an economist to recommend an austerity-oriented stabilization policy aimed at cutting the budget deficit by reducing expenditures, and then leave it to government to handle the resulting decrease in aggregate output and increase in general unemployment. Such shock therapy obviously causes economic anguish and its success depends on the willingness of political forces to tolerate these transitional costs.[20]

Already there are signs that the populace may be unwilling to pay the price for drastic free market reforms. In Lithuania, for example, where industrial production tumbled 48.5 percent in 1991, where one-third of all factories closed or sharply cut back employment, where consumer prices jumped 2,200 percent since 1990, and where fuel was in such short supply that central heating plants shut off hot water to most homes, what happened? In November 1992, the people voted to put the

[19] David Lipton and Jeffrey Sachs, "Creating a Market Economy," 99.

[20] This is the point made by Zbiginiev Brzezinski. Interview, *Moscow News Weekly*, no. 27, July 5–12, 1992. See also John Feffer, *Shock Waves* (Boston: South End Press, 1992).

former communists back into power to restore economic order and stability.[21]

Given these political realities, might it not be preferable, therefore, to follow a gradual, step-by-step approach rather than trying to impose a radical reform program all at once?[22]

ADVISOR: Gradualism may seem to be a low-risk strategy, but the chances of masterminding an economywide "soft landing" is a mirage and illusion. A gradualist solution, as Rudiger Dornbush wisely observed, is appropriate once a market economy is in place—where the issue is how to improve the use of resources at the margin. But that is not the case in Eastern Europe. That is why radical, rapid, and comprehensive reform is the right medicine. Speed is of the essence because the ice is melting, there is a lot of it to cross, and the task is overwhelming.

PRIME MINISTER: Lenin once remarked that the transition from capitalism to socialism does not pose a problem. Any cook, he said, can be taught to administer a socialist economy. Whatever the validity of that claim, I don't think it applies to our transition problems. A market economy is a world of accountants, stockbrokers, investment planners, and financial wizards. It takes time for cooks to become MBAs, and longer still to become entrepreneurs and innovators.

---

[21] Allen Cooperman, Associated Press Report, Nov. 16, 1992.

[22] On this issue, see, e.g., Kevin M. Murphy, Andrei Shleifer, and Robert W. Vishny, "The Transition to a Market Economy: Pitfalls of Partial Reform," *Quarterly Journal of Economics* 107 (Aug. 1992): 889ff., and Anthony Y. C. Koo, Elizabeth H. Li, and Peng Zhao-ping, "The Role of State-Owned Enterprises in Economic Transition," in Walter Galenson, ed., *China's Economic Reform* forthcoming.

ADVISOR: The OECD has wrestled with this issue and, on the basis of its extensive experience, reached the following conclusion: "While a gradualist approach may cause lesser social tensions, a long period of moderate reforms entails the danger that both reformers and the population will 'become tired of reforms,' as they do not seem to bring visible changes. Also during a long period of reforms various anti-reform and other lobbies may mobilize their forces and may gradually strangle the reform process."[23] The shock treatment makes sense because the public tolerance for sacrifice is brief and the courage of politicians is limited. A gradual adjustment runs the risk of being undermined by a coalescence of special interest groups, which may succeed in derailing the reforms—or eviscerating them, one by one.

PRIME MINISTER: There is some evidence, throughout the region, to support your contention. At the outset of the reform process, people were willing to take a plunge into opaque waters, not knowing where the bottom was and how long they would have to hold their breath. They were willing to make some sacrifices in the short run, believing that their lives would be better in the long run. Now, after only a few years of the reform process, they are beginning to have doubts. The miracles they expected from the market have, in most cases, not yet been realized. The people are getting restless, and the politicians are losing their nerve. Interest groups are locked in an unstructured free-for-

---

[23] OECD, *Transition from the Command to a Market Economy* (Paris: OECD, 1990), 9. See also Sylvia Nasar, "Russians Urged to Act Fast," *New York Times*, Jan. 6, 1992.

all: pensioners demanding increased benefits, the newly unemployed asking for security, plant managers seeking continued subsidies to keep their businesses alive, nationalists attacking foreign investment, and the hopelessly splintered political parties mired in unending gridlock. Everywhere there are demands to attenuate the transition costs of implementing the Big Bang. Under the circumstances, how long do you think democratic governments can stay on course?

ADVISOR: Are you suggesting that autocratic governments would have an easier time imposing the necessary reforms—that there may be a conflict between market economics and democratic politics?

PRIME MINISTER: No. I'm simply pointing out the tensions that develop when a society tries to restructure its economy and its political system simultaneously.

ADVISOR: Such tensions are unavoidable, and even predictable, but they should not be allowed to vitiate the implementation of shock therapy. You must be mindful of the fact that piecemeal reform of an internally consistent economic system may make things worse rather than better. Any single reform (or perhaps any limited set of promarket reforms) may aggravate the difficulties of a command economy. The reason is that socialist states have evolved a set of rules, incentives, and expectations designed to optimize economic performance within the confines of a command economy. Changing any rule, however sensible the change might be in the framework of a mature market economy, may lead to distortions that worsen performance in the partially reformed command economy. William Nordhaus makes this point with a biological metaphor: "No one doubts that a fish swims better than a dog. But dogs do swim in their own funny way. And replacing a dog's legs with a fish tail, in a step-by-step reform of canine navigation, would quickly produce one sad pup."[24]

PRIME MINISTER: [*Flipping to the last chart on the easel*] Let's summarize this discussion by examining Chart 8, which presents the arguments for the Big Bang model, as opposed to the case for gradual reform.

ADVISOR: That's an eminently fair summary of the conflicting policy alternatives.

PRIME MINISTER: Let me ask you a final question. Can capitalism overcome its seemingly inherent instability—the cyclical fluctuations between prosperity and depression, the alternate occurrence of inflation and unemployment? Can a market economy guarantee a minimum standard of living for everyone?

ADVISOR: The answer is obviously positive. Since the 1930s, most capitalist countries have demonstrated their ability to moderate the scourges of the business cycle and to provide basic material security for the people. They have done this in a world in which billions of people suffer from material deprivation.

Governments that want to eradicate poverty while minimizing losses of efficiency are not helpless in capitalist economies. The social democratic model is clearly viable. Irrationality in capitalism is not a given. Governments elected with a mandate to assure everyone of material security do have instruments with which to pursue their mission.

PRIME MINISTER: That's why, like Arthur Okun, I am prepared to give "two cheers for the market, but not three."

[24] Nordhaus, "Stabilizing," 300–301.

CHART 8. THE BIG BANG MODEL VERSUS GRADUALISM

Big Bang Model	Gradualism
1. *End-point driven.* Choice of initial policy determined by the goal for the final outcome of the process.	*Focus on immediate problem.* Identifies worst problems, trying to solve them, largely ignoring the effects of today's decisions on some longrun equilibrium.
2. *Clean the slate.* Emphasizes the interrelatedness of society's problems and therefore the need to make a decisive break with the past, with the necessity of institutional destruction in the first stages.	*Use existing institutions.* Recognizes that new structures can be created only slowly and accepts that existing institutions are usually better than either none or hastily constructed alternatives.
3. *Large leaps.* To make a decisive break from the constraints of the past, advocates bold policy steps that involve packages of many new institutions.	*Small steps.* Emphasizes the risks from going too fast and the impossibility of successfully creating a network of interrelated institutions anew.
4. *Faith in the new.* Willingness to trust in theoretical reasoning as the primary input for the design of society's new arrangements.	*Skepticism.* Searches for existing models and methods to help in the formulation of institutional changes.
5. *Irreversibility.* In the weak form, willingness to accept large irreversible changes. In the strong form, emphasizes the need for them.	*Reversibility.* Advocates policies that facilitate feedback on their effects and that can be stopped or even reversed.
6. *Design and theory.* The most important intellectual resource for policy-makers is the knowledge held by theoreticians and technocrats.	*Judgment and practice.* The most important intellectual resource is the practical experience accumulated in the context of a particular set of institutional arrangements.

Source: Adapted from Peter Murrell, "Conservative Political Philosophy and the Strategy of Economic Transition," *East European Politics and Societies* 6 (Winter 1992): 13.

ADVISOR: That's a tribute to my powers of persuasion. Thank you!

PRIME MINISTER: Perhaps the greatest encomium to capitalism appears in the *Communist Manifesto*, where Marx and Engels describe it as an unrivaled engine of economic growth: "[T]he bourgeoisie, during its rule of scarce one hundred years, has created more massive and more colossal productive forces than have all preceding generations together. Subjection of Nature's forces to man, machinery, application of chemistry to industry and agriculture, steam-navigation, railways, electric telegraphs, clearing of whole continents for cultivation, canalization of rivers, whole populations conjured out of the ground—what earlier century had even a presentiment that such productive forces slumbered in the lap of social labor?"[25]

ADVISOR: I couldn't have said it better myself.

PRIME MINISTER: On that conciliatory note, let us adjourn until tomorrow.

[25] Karl Marx and Friedrich Engels, *The Communist Manifesto* (1848; reprint Baltimore: Penguin, 1967), 85.

DAY 6 – GOVERNMENT AND
THE MARKET

---

*The U.S. case illuminates the government-market interface.
The conferees discuss public health and safety, rapaciousness,
negative externalities and market remedies, disparities of
political clout and capture of the political process, armies,
and the safety net in the modern welfare state.*

PRIME MINISTER: Our discussions thus far have focused
primarily on the market system, private enterprise, and
the freedom of individuals to make economic decisions. But we must also consider the duty of the state
to protect the health, safety, and general welfare of the
citizenry.

ADVISOR: On this point, I am a firm believer in Thomas
Jefferson's maxim: The government governs best that
governs least.

PRIME MINISTER: That doesn't mean anarchy. I, too,
have read Adam Smith. In *The Wealth of Nations*, the
bible of free enterprise, he outlined the roles that government must play in a market system: "first, the duty
of protecting the society from the violence and invasion
of other independent societies; secondly, the duty of
protecting, as far as possible, every member of the society from the injustice or oppression of every other
member of it, or the duty of establishing an exact administration of justice; and, thirdly, the duty of erect-
ing and maintaining certain public works and certain
public institutions, which it can never be for the in-

terest of any individual, or small number of individuals, to erect and maintain; because the profit could never repay the expense to any individual or small number of individuals, though it may frequently do much more than repay it to a great society" (p. 651).

ADVISOR: Remember that Adam Smith, in the same "bible," also said that the "statesman, who should attempt to direct private people in what manner they ought to employ their capitals, would not only load himself with a most unnecessary attention, but assume an authority which could safely be trusted, not only to no single person, but to no council or senate whatever, and which would nowhere be so dangerous as in the hands of a man who had folly and presumption enough to fancy himself fit to exercise it" (p. 423).

PRIME MINISTER: True enough. But a close reading reveals that Adam Smith was no laissez-faire ideologue: He saw that self-interest and market competition are sometimes treacherous; that it may be necessary for government to engage in activities across a broad front, where the need can be shown and the competence of government can be demonstrated; and that these instances must be objectively evaluated on a case-by-case basis.[1] In other words, Adam Smith recognized that government has a responsibility for correcting market system imperfections.

ADVISOR: Fine. But before we get into specifics, you must understand that while market imperfections may occur, government imperfections occur just as often, if

[1] See the chapter "Adam Smith and Laissez Faire," in Jacob Viner, *The Long View and the Short: Studies in Economic Theory and Policy* (Glencoe, Ill.: The Free Press, 1958), esp. 228–45.

not oftener, with consequences just as undesirable, if not worse.

Moreover, we must be aware of what might be called the "reverse invisible hand" problem: In private economic affairs, people attempting to pursue their own self-interest are led as if by an invisible hand to promote the public interest. But in the political sphere, the opposite occurs; individuals attempting to pursue their conception of the public interest are led by an invisible hand to produce undesirable results that it is no part of their intention to promote.[2] The theory of public choice teaches that government action is congenitally afflicted by voter ignorance, the capture of mercenary politicians by special interest groups, and a lack of incentives for efficiency. Thus, while the private market may be imperfect, government suffers from its own peculiar foibles and deficiencies.

PRIME MINISTER: Are you quite sure the invisible hand never goes awry? never needs restraint? Isn't it a question of balance? Let's take consumer protection, for example. We are familiar with your famous consumer advocate, Ralph Nader, and his crusade for consumer protection. Given that your market economy is long-established, while ours is only in its infancy, it seems especially incumbent upon us to enact laws and establish government agencies to protect our newly liberated consumers.

ADVISOR: You are terribly mistaken. It is the market that protects consumers, and it does so better than any laws or government bureaucrats. Your good intentions will

[2] Milton Friedman, "From Galbraith to Economic Freedom," (Institute of Economic Affairs, 1977), 35.

only produce an inefficient nanny state, extending into every nook and cranny of your people's lives.

PRIME MINISTER: Why is that?

ADVISOR: The flawed premise of the consumer protection crusade by Ralph Nader and other so-called "reformers" is that unless the government moves into the marketplace with hordes of agencies and inspectors, consumers will be preyed upon by rapacious sellers. But the fundamental fact is that if a consumer is being sold rotten meat at the grocery store, he or she has the very best consumer protection agency available—the market. The consumer simply stops patronizing that store, and switches to another. The grocer selling rotten meat will lose sales and suffer financial losses. The free market thus will force the grocer to sell good meat or go out of business.[3]

PRIME MINISTER: Isn't the problem more complex than that? What if the consumer is incapable of judging the hazard posed by some products? After all, even in your sophisticated nation, not everyone has advanced degrees in engineering, chemistry, or bioanatomy.

ADVISOR: Don't underestimate the value of brand names to a producer. It is in a producer's own interest to obtain a reputation for making dependable, reliable products. Indeed, this reputation may be far more valuable to a firm than any of its plants and factories.[4]

PRIME MINISTER: Do you mean firms such as A. H. Robins, which marketed the Dalkon Shield intrauterine birth control device, despite the company's knowl-

---

[3] Milton Friedman, *Bright Promises, Dismal Performance* (New York: Harcourt, Brace Jovanovich, 1983), 21.

[4] Milton Friedman and Rose Friedman, *Free to Choose* (New York: Avon Books, 1980), 213.

edge that the product was dangerous, and continued to market it after it had maimed and infected thousands of women?[5] Or Upjohn, which marketed the Halcion sleeping pill, while concealing evidence that the drug causes serious psychiatric side effects?[6] What about Dow Corning, which marketed silicone gel breast implants, while repeatedly postponing tests to determine their safety despite physician complaints of seriously adverse patient reactions?[7]

ADVISOR: Of course, mistakes will happen.[8]

PRIME MINISTER: Such systematic patterns of deliberate deception hardly seem to warrant such an easy way out. In the case of the Dalkon Shield, for example, Judge Lord found that A. H. Robins, "without warning to women, invaded their bodies by the millions and caused them injuries by the thousands," that the firm was "collectively being enriched by millions of dollars each year," and that Robins "continued to allow women, tens of thousands of them, to wear a device—a deadly depth charge in their wombs, ready to explode at any time."[9]

ADVISOR: Perfection is not of this world! There will always be shoddy products, quacks, and con artists. But when it is permitted to work, market competition pro-

---

[5] See Morton Mintz, *At Any Cost: Corporate Greed, Women, and the Dalkon Shield* (New York: Pantheon Books, 1985).

[6] Gina Kolata, "Maker of Sleeping Pill Hid Data on Side Effects, Researchers Say," *New York Times*, Jan. 20, 1992, 1.

[7] Philip J. Hilts, "Maker is Depicted as Fighting Tests on Implant Safety," *New York Times*, Jan. 13, 1992, 1.

[8] Friedman and Friedman, *Free to Choose*, 198.

[9] Quoted in Sheldon Engelmayer and Robert Wagner, *Lord's Justice* (Garden City, N.Y.: Anchor Press, 1985), 256–58.

tects the consumer better than do government restraints imposed upon the market.[10]

PRIME MINISTER: But without some kind of consumer safeguards, how can our people be protected from the kind of harm I've just described?[11]

ADVISOR: What you have to understand is that government regulation is subject to peculiar laws of its own: it moves in bizarre directions that have little relation to its original intention.[12] U.S. auto safety regulations, for example, have actually reduced automotive safety by encouraging drivers to behave more recklessly.[13] So you see, government regulations intended to make products safer may only harm consumers.

PRIME MINISTER: This logic seems to imply that automakers should pack the interiors of their cars with razor blades and broken glass in order to encourage drivers to behave cautiously. Wouldn't it make more common sense to prevent harm in advance—and also be more economical than dealing with the kind of massive, time-consuming, and expensive litigation your U.S. firms constantly bewail?

ADVISOR: When products freely enter the market there is an opportunity for trial and error. Consumers can experiment for themselves. They can decide what features they like and what features they don't like. But when government steps in, the situation is drastically altered. Now decisions have to be made before the prod-

---

[10] Friedman and Friedman, *Free to Choose*, 212.
[11] See David Bollier and Joan Claybrook, *Freedom from Harm* (Washington, D.C.: Public Citizen, 1986).
[12] Friedman and Friedman, *Free to Choose*, 183.
[13] Sam Peltzman, "The Effects of Automobile Safety Regulation," *Journal of Political Economy* 83 (Aug. 1975): 677–718.

uct is tested in actual use. Government regulatory standards can't be adjusted to different consumer needs and tastes, but instead must be uniformly applied to all. Consumers will be deprived of their freedom to experiment with a complete range of alternatives. Competing sources of supply protect the consumer far better than all the Ralph Naders in the world.

PRIME MINISTER: But where people's lives, health, and personal safety are at stake, what you call "freedom to choose" seems tantamount to freedom to play Russian roulette. Surely you would concede that ensuring the competence of physicians and surgeons, for example, requires some kind of regulatory certification.

ADVISOR: Absolutely not. I have long recommended that physician licensure be abolished as a requirement for practicing medicine.[14]

PRIME MINISTER: Would you deny that some type of government agency is required to regulate the safety of foods and medicines?

ADVISOR: I deny that water runs uphill! I deny that you can have cats that bark like dogs! Your claim contradicts the fundamental nature of things! Tough drug regulations enacted in the United States in the early 1960s only served to reduce the rate of introduction of new drugs by pharmaceutical firms; the belief that they did anything else is misguided. How does that outcome promote the public interest? How does it promote consumer welfare? The U.S. Food and Drug Administration should be abolished![15]

---

[14] Milton Friedman, *Capitalism and Freedom* (Chicago: University of Chicago Press, 1962), 158.

[15] Friedman, *Bright Promises*, 22–23; Friedman and Friedman, *Free to Choose*, 195–99.

PRIME MINISTER: An alternative interpretation would be that those regulations have been highly effective, by preventing the marketing of dangerous drugs and medicines that have no demonstrable therapeutic benefits.[16] But enough of drugs. What about airline safety? In an unregulated free market, how could travelers possibly evaluate the safety of a particular carrier—the soundness of its craft; its performance of essential repairs, maintenance, and servicing; the competence and sobriety of its pilots?

ADVISOR: Like any other product or service, airline safety is regulated by the basic market motivation to make money. Most air travelers are risk averse, meaning most prefer to avoid accidents and are willing to reduce their chances of accidents. Airline managers understand that accidents, and the injuries and fatalities that result from them, translate into lost business and lower profits.[17]

PRIME MINISTER: [*After conversing with a deputy*] If that's so, how do you explain the fact that in the late 1980s a number of your airlines were fined record amounts by the Federal Aeronautics Administration for failing to perform essential maintenance and repairs on their aircraft, and for falsifying their equipment service records?[18]

---

[16] See Douglas F. Greer, *Industrial Organization and Public Policy* (New York: Macmillan, 1980), 654–57.

[17] Richard B. McKenzie, "Airline Deregulation and Air-Travel Safety," (Center for the Study of American Business, Publication no. 107, July 1991), 32.

[18] See Philip Shenon, "Eastern to Pay $9.5 Million Airline Safety Fine," *New York Times*, Feb. 11, 1987, 1, 24; Paulette Thomas, "Continental Air to Be Studied by U.S. Agency," *Wall Street Journal*, Apr. 18, 1988, 3; Laurie McGinley, "*Pan Am to Pay $2 Million Fine in Safety Case*," ibid., Aug. 25,

ADVISOR: I would point out that some of those air carriers have since gone bankrupt. The most effective deterrent a producer can feel is the loss of profits. It will be careful about what it puts on the market because it doesn't want to lose business. As the Council of Economic Advisors to former President Ronald Reagan has stressed, market incentives will lead manufacturers to produce products as safe as consumers demand.[19]

PRIME MINISTER: But suppose manufacturers prevent consumers from exercising their freedom to choose when it comes to product safety? For example, your Big Three auto companies battled against air bags for decades. They did everything in their power to stymie rules requiring air bags and to dissuade consumers from purchasing automobiles equipped with them—despite evidence that installation of air bags would save thousands of lives, and despite their own surveys revealing half or more of their buyers' willingness to pay sizable additional amounts for air bag protection.[20] In these circumstances, how can you be so confident about producers automatically responding to consumer "willingness to pay"?

ADVISOR: We have to look at the real world. I think that

1986, 2; Richard Witkin, "600,775 Fine Sought against Airline," *New York Times*, Jan. 16, 1985, 7; id., "FAA Seeks to Fine American Airlines for Use of 'Improper Parts,'" ibid., Jan. 17, 1985, 7; Christopher Conte, "U.S. Inspection of Airlines Led to Restrictions," *Wall Street Journal*, Dec. 13, 1984 2.

[19] *Economic Report of the President, 1987*, 193.

[20] See Peter Passell, "What's Holding Back Air Bags?" *New York Times Magazine*, Dec. 18, 1983, 75; United Services Automobile Association, *Aide Magazine*, Summer 1985, 13–14; *Wall Street Journal*, Nov. 11, 1976, 1; Albert R. Carr and Laurie McGinley, "Auto Shoppers Encounter Stiff Resistance When Seeking Air Bags at Ford Dealers," *Wall Street Journal*, July 31, 1986, 23.

as consumers we do pretty well if government leaves us alone.[21]

PRIME MINISTER: What about banking and financial markets? The freewheeling, devil-may-care practices engaged in by our fledgling banking sector, for example, are raising grave concerns that many of our banks may collapse.[22] Isn't there a critical need for banking laws like the ones your country enacted in the 1930s to prevent a recurrence of the financial catastrophes caused by the razzle-dazzle bank deals and stock market frauds of the Roaring Twenties?[23]

ADVISOR: That's largely a myth. The failure of a bank is really no more significant than the failure of any other economic organization; in fact, in many respects, it is less significant. I consider most of the rationales given for bank regulation to be theoretically incorrect and irrelevant.[24]

PRIME MINISTER: People whose life savings would be wiped out by bank failures would hardly consider their loss to be irrelevant.

ADVISOR: Of course, deposits must be insured in order to protect individuals from such losses. But there is no reason why government must monopolize this function. The private sector can provide deposit insurance

---

[21] Friedman, *Bright Promises*, 165.

[22] Louis Uchitelle, "The Roulette of Russian Banking," *New York Times*, Feb. 29, 1992, 17.

[23] For surveys, see John Kenneth Galbraith, *The Great Crash: 1929* (Boston: Houghton Mifflin, 1954), and Ferdinand Pecora, *Wall Street under Oath* (reprint, New York: Augustus M. Kelley, 1968).

[24] See testimony of George J. Benston in U.S. Congress, Senate, Committee on Banking, Housing, and Urban Affairs, *Hearings on Competitive Equity in the Financial Services Industry*, 98th Cong., 2d sess., 1984, 1040–1104.

for banks, just as it provides insurance coverage for other kinds of risks. Thus, I advocate free entry into banking by anyone, provided only that they have obtained sufficient deposit insurance.

PRIME MINISTER: The S & L fiasco in your country seems to refute your confidence in unregulated bank markets. Looted by rogues, charlatans, and outright thieves in what has been called the greatest financial heist in history, the S & Ls have saddled U.S. taxpayers with a bill of three hundred to five hundred billion dollars to clean up the mess![25]

ADVISOR: To the contrary, I would argue that the S & L affair confirms my point. It was partial deregulation that caused the problem. While savings and loan institutions were freed to engage in all kinds of investments outside their traditional field of home mortgage lending, at the same time they continued to benefit from government deposit protection. This encouraged them to take unwarranted risks, because they had nothing to lose, knowing that the full faith and credit of the government stood ready to rescue their depositors should their risky ventures fail.

PRIME MINISTER: That's a persuasive point, but now let's move on to another area. What about environmental pollution—the degradation of air, water, land, and possibly even the earth's protective ozone layer? Doesn't environmental pollution constitute what economists call a negative externality? Doesn't it result because profit-maximizing decisions made by individuals

[25] See Stephen Pizzo, Mary Fricker, and Paul Muolo, *Inside Job: The Looting of America's Savings and Loans* (New York: McGraw-Hill, 1989), and Lawrence J. White, *The S & L Debacle* (New York: Oxford University Press, 1991).

and organizations damage others, producing harmful consequences not taken into account by those making the decisions? For example, it is profit maximizing for an enterprise to dispose of its toxic wastes by simply dumping them out the back door. But the surrounding community does not relish being poisoned in this fashion.

ADVISOR: I'll grant you that negative externalities, such as environmental pollution, are a problem for a market economy. However, discussions of the environment are fraught with emotion rather than reason. The fact is that there is no such thing as a free lunch—if we want less pollution, a price must be paid in the form of less economic growth, less job generation, and so forth. How much of the latter are we willing to trade off for the former?—that's the core question that must be confronted.

PRIME MINISTER: It seems to me that your premise for framing the pollution problem presents a false trade-off between environment and production: A number of firms in your country are finding that redesigning their production operations, and reducing the pollutants *before* they have been produced, not only protects the environment but also dramatically boosts corporate productivity and efficiency.[26] Rather than conflicting with efficient production, environmentally safe operating methods may actually promote it, in which case there really is no trade-off. It is also interesting to note that Japanese manufacturers—who face some of the world's strictest pollution laws—are developing into a

[26] See Amal Naj, "Some Companies Cut Pollution by Altering Production Methods," *Wall Street Journal*, Dec. 24, 1990, 1.

major export industry the pollution control technologies their government has forced them to implement.[27]

ADVISOR: Voilà! Again, the market works!

PRIME MINISTER: Doesn't government have responsibility for imposing some limits on the discretion of private property owners to pursue profit to the detriment of the environment?

ADVISOR: Of course it does. But the pollution problem is not unique to an economy based on private property and the pursuit of profit. After all, look at the horrible ecological devastation wrought by decades of your communist economic control.[28] In Poland, acid rain has so corroded railroad tracks that trains are not allowed to exceed twenty-four miles per hour; contamination of farmland with heavy metals has reached epidemic proportions; and water is so foul that it destroys industrial machinery.[29]

PRIME MINISTER: Yes, our record is shameful. But you haven't really answered my question: doesn't government have to limit property owners' discretion to pollute?

ADVISOR: Not in the sense that regulations forbidding pollution are necessary. As Nobel laureate Ronald Coase demonstrated in his classic article, the environmental pollution problem occurs because private property rights are not defined, and because voluntary

---

[27] Neil Gross, "The Green Giant? It May Be Japan," *Business Week*, Feb. 24, 1992, 74–75.

[28] See Murray Feshback and Alfred Friendly, *Ecocide in the USSR* (New York: Basic Books, 1992).

[29] See Robert J. Smith, "Privatizing the Environment," *Policy Review*, Spring 1982, 11–14; and Marlise Simons, "Investors Shy Away from Polluted Eastern Europe," *New York Times*, May 13, 1992, 1.

exchange through the private market is precluded from solving the problem.[30]

PRIME MINISTER: What do you mean?

ADVISOR: Consider the case of a factory that destroys fish by polluting a stream. Suppose the Izaak Walton League were assigned property rights to the stream. In order to dump its wastes, the factory then would have to pay the League to use its property; the factory would have to compensate it for its loss of fish. If the value to the factory of the stream as a waste dump exceeded the value of the stream as a fishing source, then a voluntary, mutually beneficial bargain would be struck: The League would freely choose to abandon its use of the stream in return for sufficient financial compensation by the factory.

PRIME MINISTER: But what if the League valued the stream at more than what the factory was willing to pay?

ADVISOR: Then it would simply refuse to accept financial compensation, and the stream would be utilized for fishing. In fact, Professor Coase showed that it doesn't matter who is initially assigned property rights in the stream. So long as ownership is defined clearly, and is transferable, those who value the resource most will pay the most to use it. Regardless of who is assigned ownership initially, the market will direct the use of the stream into the hands of those who value it the most.[31]

PRIME MINISTER: It certainly makes a difference in

[30] Ronald H. Coase, "The Problem of Social Cost," *Journal of Law and Economics*, 3 (Oct. 1960): 1.

[31] Steven N. S. Cheung, *The Myth of Social Cost* (Washington, D.C.: Cato Institute, 1980), 58–59.

terms of who pays whom—whose income is enhanced and whose is reduced! It also makes a difference in terms of who has the greater ability to pay to avoid damage, or to purchase the property rights. How do you suggest we go about the business of enforcing "ownership" of the air our people breathe, or shielding the ozone layer that protects them from ultraviolet rays? Should we float signs in the air stating *Private Property—Trespassers Will Be Prosecuted*? How could millions of our people be assembled and brought to agreement on a mutually acceptable bargain?

ADVISOR: Admittedly, the approach may not work in all cases, but it deserves serious consideration. Government's role can be generally shaped along the lines of facilitating private market solutions to the pollution problem, rather than concocting costly, counterproductive interventionist approaches.

PRIME MINISTER: Could you provide an example?

ADVISOR: Certainly. Consider the use of effluent fees: Instead of government regulations dictating the precise pollution control techniques and equipment that firms must install, you simply impose a fee, or price, per unit of pollution emitted. You thus "internalize" the externality. You give polluters the choice of whether it is cheaper for them to clean up their operations and avoid paying the fee. But you leave producers free to choose whether to pollute or not; if the latter, you let them choose the most efficient way of cleaning up their operations. A variant of this approach, promoted by then-President George Bush, was included in the U.S. Clean Air Act of 1990: the issuance of permits to pollute, which could be bought and sold for a price.[32]

[32] See *Economic Report of the President, 1990*, 187–97; and Richard W.

PRIME MINISTER: Permits to pollute! Should we also sell permits to murder? Wouldn't these encourage the optimum amount of homicide?

ADVISOR: You can make light of the idea if you wish. The fact remains that these are ways that market incentives of profit and loss can be substituted for burdensome, expensive and ineffective government command-and-control regulations.

PRIME MINISTER: What about national defense? Isn't this a classic case of what economists call a public good? Isn't it something that once provided for some, is available to all, whether or not they pay for it? Doesn't this create a serious "free rider" problem, where each person relies on others to pay for it and, as a result, no one contributes, even though all agree it is needed? As Adam Smith pointed out, mustn't government provide defense through compulsory tax contributions?

ADVISOR: Economists used to think so. However, there may be other alternatives. A recent study contends that pre–nineteenth century privateers—private operators licensed by governments to capture enemy ships, to confiscate and sell their cargo, and to retain a share of the proceeds—provided an economically superior means for national defense during wartime. This was less wasteful because privateers kept ships and cargoes rather than sinking them. It also was more efficient, because in peacetime governments avoided the ex-

---

Stevenson, "Trying a Market Approach to Smog," *New York Times*, Mar. 25, 1992, C1.

pense of mothballing navies; the privateers were simply released from contract.[33]

PRIME MINISTER: Wonderful—thugs armed to the teeth, released to ravage the world at will! I'm sure Saddam Hussein and Colonel Khaddafi would relish the prospect of privatizing our nuclear arsenal!

ADVISOR: Admittedly, the suggestion may be extreme. Nevertheless, there is no denying the fact that, even as we speak, a "rent-a-tank" market is flourishing in some republics of the former Soviet Union. Obviously, the private sector cannot be ignored, even in the national defense arena.

PRIME MINISTER: What about the need for a generalized social safety net? Under socialism, there was no unemployment because state enterprise kept thousands of redundant workers on their payroll. They also provided employees and their families with a panoply of cradle-to-grave social services: housing and meals, clinics and hospitals, schools and day-care centers, recreational facilities and virtually free vacation cottages. At times they even provided road construction for local communities. But with privatization and marketization, state enterprises will no longer be financially capable of providing such safety nets. The wrenching economic transformation we are planning will therefore impose unprecedented economic hardship on our people: skyrocketing prices for food, shelter, energy, and clothing; massive layoffs and shutdowns of hope-

---

[33] Gary M. Anderson and Adam Gifford, Jr., "Privateering and the Private Production of Naval Power," *Cato Journal*, Spring/Summer 1991, 99–122.

lessly obsolete plants and factories; unemployment, homelessness, and hunger.

ADVISOR: Some of my colleagues feel strongly that a social safety net is indispensable in order to ensure that the burdens of economic transformation aren't unfairly distributed and that they don't undermine the social consensus for change.[34] Like them, I recognize that the weaning of state enterprises from government subsidies and easy credit, the pressures imposed on managers to cut costs and increase efficiency, the introduction of competition, and the elimination of inflation will generate large increases in unemployment, which must be addressed if economic restructuring is to progress.[35] In other words, there is need for a safety net to deal with temporary, transitional unemployment. In meeting this need, however, you must exercise extreme caution not to create a welfare state that promotes a permanent "underclass." Here, I believe, the law of supply and demand is capable of doing great damage.

PRIME MINISTER: What do you mean?

ADVISOR: To put it bluntly and crudely, the danger is that where a demand for poor people is created, the supply of them will expand to meet the demand.

PRIME MINISTER: Who in their right mind would create a demand for poor people?

ADVISOR: I'm afraid governments do. No matter how well

[34] David Lipton and Jeffrey Sachs, "Creating a Market Economy in Eastern Europe: The Case of Poland," *Brookings Papers on Economic Activity* 1 (1990): 125.

[35] Merton J. Peck and Thomas J. Richardson, eds., *What Is to Be Done? Proposals for the Soviet Transition to the Market* (New Haven: Yale University Press, 1991), 33; Olivier Blanchard et al., *Reform in Eastern Europe* (Cambridge, Mass: MIT Press, 1991), 90.

intentioned, overly generous welfare programs run the risk of unintentionally creating a "demand" for those who qualify for the benefits the programs provide.[36]

PRIME MINISTER: The alternative seems extraordinarily cruel.

ADVISOR: In the short run it may appear cruel, but in the long run it is far more humane than creating an expanding, permanent "underclass" of welfare dependents drained of their initiative, their self-esteem, and their self-confidence.

PRIME MINISTER: But as my Russian friends say, an empty sack can't stand up. People must eat. They must have heat to avoid freezing to death. They must have medical care when they're ill.

ADVISOR: As a temporary palliative, yes. But people must eventually become responsible for themselves and for their own welfare. This is the great attraction of the market system. It releases people's energies and talents. It provides mobility. It creates opportunities for the disadvantaged of today to become the well-to-do of tomorrow. In the process, it enables everyone, from top to bottom, to enjoy a fuller and richer life. I believe history demonstrates that an overly generous government safety net often is the first step down the slippery slope to a welfare state and a coercive society.

PRIME MINISTER: I'm beginning to think you are an anarchist after all.

ADVISOR: Remember, Karl Marx said that communism would be characterized by the withering away of the state. Does that make me a Marxist? Perhaps, in my

---

[36] Charles Murray, *Losing Ground* (New York: Basic Books, 1984), 212–16.

effort to warn you against the menace of a wasteful, overblown, counterproductive welfare state, I have articulated an unduly extreme position—a point of view, incidentally, that a good many of my colleagues in the American Economic Association would reject as utopian and impractical. Nevertheless, I think it is useful advice for the countries in your region as they struggle to create their market economies and to rid themselves of pervasive state direction and control.[37]

PRIME MINISTER: Aren't you exaggerating the role of laissez-faire in a market economy? Isn't it true that, over the years, whether Republicans or Democrats, conservatives or liberals, were in power, the United States has had a more activist government than you would prescribe for us? Isn't it true that today the United States has, and in the foreseeable future is likely to have, a predominantly free economy, in which government has responsibility for moderating unemployment and inflation, for providing defense and certain other services, for redistribution of income and the opportunity to assist the poor, and for regulation where there are major, clear cases of failure of free markets to yield socially beneficial results. How best to do these

---

[37] After studying the problems of postcommunism, Richard Rose of the University of Strathclyde offers this more balanced view on the role of the state: "In Europe, both conservatives and social democrats start from the assumption that functioning markets presuppose a civil order. It is the state, not the market, that legislates property rights. It is the state, not the market, that maintains public order, and creates the secure environment that encourages investment. The state also has explicit economic functions, such as operating a central bank and printing currency. These are not radical ideas; they were familiar to the framers of the American Constitution, and to Gladstone and Disraeli. The *Rechtstaat* (a state based on right not might) comes before profit-seeking in the market." "Toward a Civil Economy," *Journal of Democracy* 3 (Apr. 1992): 21.

things, and how far to go with them, are proper questions for discussion. But within the range of options likely to be considered none of the choices would add up to radical change from this moderate approach.[38]

ADVISOR: That's true, but as President Bill Clinton said, the trick is to know "the limits of what government can do, as well as what government must do."[39]

PRIME MINISTER: I trust we both appreciate the enormous irony in all of this. To achieve the reforms you advocate—privatizing enterprises, distributing stock ownership, restructuring factories, deconcentrating industries, enacting commercial laws, creating courts, and so forth—may require a government of almost unlimited powers. Yet the ultimate objective of the reforms is precisely the opposite: a democratic market economy where government has very limited powers. An even greater irony is that to succeed, economic transformation demands extraordinary confidence by the people in their government. Remember that it was the lack of this confidence that precipitated the overthrow of the communist regime. But today we see confidence in government once again eroded by instability, disorder, and widespread corruption.[40]

---

[38] Herbert Stein, "This Inane Campaign Gives Me a Pain," *Wall Street Journal*, Oct. 7, 1992, A14.

[39] *New York Times* (Midwestern ed.), Dec. 12, 1992, 14Y.

[40] Laurie Hays, "Russian Corruption Transcends Communist Era, Tainting Even the 'New Generation' Politicians," *Wall Street Journal*, Oct. 6, 1992, A14. In Russia, lawlessness is seemingly pervasive: this year, over 60 percent of the young men called up for military duty have failed to report; three thousand officers have been disciplined for corruption and forty-six generals currently face prosecution (*Economist*, Feb. 27, 1993: 53). Also, as President Yeltsin told a meeting of law enforcement officers, "currency speculators, money launderers, smugglers of raw materials, bribe takers and embezzlers pervade key ministries, bleeding the treasury of billions of dollars and jeop-

Perhaps we should recall what James Madison, one of the founders of your nation, said about government. In *The Federalist No. 51*, he asked "What is government itself, but the greatest of all reflections on human nature?" He pointed out that if "men were angels, no government would be necessary" Would you agree that we have government because humankind is fallible, imperfect, and at times capable of doing great harm?

ADVISOR: True. But we have to ask a further question. Which institution is better able to control this fallible, and at times evil, human nature? Is it the autonomous market system of checks and balances, of supply and demand, of self-interest pitted against self-interest? Or is it government—with its unbounded monopoly of coercion?

PRIME MINISTER: An excellent question on which to conclude our conversation today.

---

ardizing Russia's transition to a free-market economy. . . . Corruption in the organs of power and administration is literally corroding the state body of Russia from top to bottom." (*Los Angeles Times Service*, Feb. 13, 1993).

DAY 7 – INHERENT TENSIONS

Intrinsic tensions resist easy answers. The conferees discuss rent-seeking and protection of vested interests, diseconomies of scale, and the tiresome failure of life to conform to the theories of economists.

PRIME MINISTER: My friend, we've reached the final day of our discussions. I was intrigued by our conversation yesterday. I was struck by how much we have in common with your history. Like your colonial forebears two hundred years ago, we, too, have chafed under the yoke of oppressive government. Like them, we have to build a new social order to replace the arbitrary, despotic state we have overthrown. Like them, we have the unique opportunity to construct, from the ground up, a "good society"—a society based on government under law; a society based on the rights of individuals rather than the sovereignty of tyrants; a society based on the belief that improvement of the human lot is best achieved by unshackling thought, invention, enterprise, and labor from the rule of dictators.

ADVISOR: You're quite right. The world has indeed been turned upside down: The "old world" is now the new; the "new world" is now the old.

PRIME MINISTER: The central challenge confronting us is to construct a governance structure that provides for individual freedom while simultaneously ensuring that private decisionmaking will promote the public interest. In setting about this task, we appreciate the dilemmas your founders faced. We recognize that government must be strong enough to protect individual freedoms, but not so strong as to destroy them. We recognize that government must be strong enough to legislate and enforce legal rules that apply equally to all, but not so strong that it can arbitrarily change those rules or abolish them at will. We understand that representative government must be accountable and responsible to the people, and yet not vulnerable to capture by factions.

We admire the ingenious resolution of these challenges by your founders. Aware of humanity's shortcomings—an inordinate greed and insatiable lust for power—and believing that it was impossible to reform human nature, they concluded that vice could not be controlled by virtue, but that it was necessary to oppose one vice and interest with another vice and interest. Their solution was a constitution that divides governmental powers, dispersing them into separate branches and setting each branch against the others in an intricately balanced system of checks and balances to prevent a monopoly over government's coercive power.

ADVISOR: I wish more of my fellow citizens shared your appreciation for the genius of the U.S. constitutional system and the philosophy that informed it.

PRIME MINISTER: As I read Adam Smith, he advocated the competitive market as the economic analogue of such a political system. Like the U.S. Constitution, the competitive market disperses economic power and decisonmaking into many hands. Like the Constitution, the competitive market is a system of checks and balances, pitting producer against producer, and self-interest against self-interest. Like the Constitution, the competitive market is a governance system for a free society.

ADVISOR: Exactly. The free play of market forces determines the kinds and quantities of goods to be produced, the factors of production to be employed, the technologies to be utilized, and the division of distributive income shares. Individual activity is coordinated through an autonomous and impartial economic decisionmaking system, free of human control and manipulation. Free market forces harness the individual appetite for private gain and turn it to socially beneficial ends; they transmute private vice into public virtue. It's not perfect. But it's a system under which bad people can do least harm.

PRIME MINISTER: But isn't the concentration of economic power in private hands just as dangerous as concentrated governmental power? Doesn't it derange the functioning of the market and subvert its ability to produce the beneficial results you describe? Doesn't the deeply rooted human drive to obtain power, and to protect it from encroachment, afflict all economies and societies?

Economic transformation is not just a technical concept. More fundamentally, it marks a cataclysmic struggle for power—a struggle to determine who will control resources, who will allocate them, and who will employ them for what purposes. In our region, those who did well under the communist regime now doggedly obstruct our efforts to create a market economy, because they don't want to lose their clout, their elite status, and the privileges that go with it—favored access to the best goods, the best medical care, the finest homes, and the best schools for their children.[1]

Look at the ringleaders of the failed 1991 attempt to overthrow Gorbachev and the power blocs they represent: Alexander Tizyakov, president of the state enterprises, a group fiercely insistent on retaining control of state industries; Vassily Starodubtsyev, head of the collective farm chairmen, who are vehemently opposed to private property; Oleg Baklanov, chief representative of the vast military-industrial complex. Under these circumstances, what I fear is not that government will stifle industry, but that industry will stifle government and its reforms.

ADVISOR: True! As the Russians are wont to say, everybody loves the tree which gives him shelter. In technical terms, economists refer to it as the problem of rent-seeking behavior; overcoming these vested interests is a linchpin for the success of your economic transformation program.

PRIME MINISTER: Doesn't a market economy also require periodic restructuring?

ADVISOR: Absolutely. Economic conditions are constantly changing, usually in unanticipated ways. Technology changes. Prices, costs, demand, and supply constantly change. Shortages one year can be followed by surpluses the next. Methods of production change. Population demographics change, profoundly altering preferences. Some industries expand; others contract and disappear. A great strength of the market system is its

---

[1] Paul R. Gregory, "Soviet Bureaucracy and Economic Reform," in William S. Kern, ed., *From Socialism to Market Economy* (Kalamazoo, Mich.: Upjohn Institute, 1992), 77.

ability to adapt flexibly to change—in effect, to continuously restructure itself.

PRIME MINISTER: That's just the point. Rent-seeking by vested interests interferes with the restructuring that is imperative in all economies—yours as well as ours. Your market system is just as vulnerable to concentrations of private power, which, like those in my country, stubbornly resist change. These interests strive to preserve their position from erosion, but in doing so, they induce paralysis and afflict the economy with a sclerotic incapacity to adapt to change?[2]

Take the case of your giant steel firms, for example: They failed to implement state-of-the-art improvements in production technology. They became inefficient and uncompetitive, and fell behind the rest of the world. So what did they do? Did they sacrifice themselves on the altar of private enterprise? Did they accept their losses as the market's penalty for poor decisionmaking? Hardly. They preferred to lobby the government to obtain import restraints in order to neutralize more efficient competition.

Or consider your Chrysler Corporation. When the firm confronted bankruptcy in the late 1970s because it had failed to adopt advanced manufacturing techniques and products, did it passively resign itself to the judgment of the autonomous market? Did it meekly submit to the textbook commandments of laissez-faire economics? By no means. Instead, Chrysler unleashed a massive lobbying campaign and obtained a billion-

---

[2] See Mancur Olson, *The Rise and Decline of Nations* (New Haven: Yale University Press, 1982).

dollar government bailout—the ultimate perversion of private enterprise.[3]

Don't these examples indicate that even a market system is not immune to capture by powerful vested interests, cemented to the status quo, and capable of successfully resisting restructuring? Don't these examples demonstrate that the battle for restructuring must be waged constantly, even in a market economy?

ADVISOR: Yes, as Henry Simons warned long ago, capture of government by vested economic interests produces all the afflictions of socialism but none of its benefits.[4] I believe, however, that it is government involvement that is primarily responsible for the results you describe. Absent the interventionist state, I believe such resistance would quickly dissipate.

PRIME MINISTER: Does that mean that you are opposed to democracy and glasnost?

ADVISOR: Of course not.

PRIME MINISTER: Yet, you seem to blame government as the root of the problem. Your country is a representative democracy, designed to make the government responsive to the citizens. And so it is: when lobbied by the steel industry, the nuclear power industry, or the automobile industry, it responds in the counterproductive ways I've just described. What you imply as the solution to the problem is to somehow render government less responsive to the people, to somehow render

[3] For further analysis of these and related problems, see Walter Adams and James W. Brock, *The Bigness Complex: Industry, Labor, and Government in the American Economy* (New York: Pantheon Books, 1986).

[4] Henry C. Simons, *Economic Policy for a Free Society* (Chicago: University of Chicago Press, 1948), 87–88.

it less accountable to them—in a word, to make it more despotic.

ADVISOR: Democratic governments respond to their constituents. In a narrow sense, this is desirable. The problem in the larger sense is the conflict among interests, the disparities in clout, and the burgeoning state protectionism that result. What's called for is a constitutional order—an overarching set of political rules and restraints—capable of constraining vested interests and deflecting their debilitating machinations. In this, you, and we, must raise our sights above the confines of self-interested behavior played out within an existing politicoeconomic "constitution," even if doing so may not fit within a narrowly construed rational choice calculus. You, and we, must devise new constitutional structures that are better able to prevent the intrusion of politics into market exchange. Because you are starting from scratch in building your political, economic and social structures, your postcommunist society has a unique opportunity to lead the way in this endeavor for the rest of us.[5]

PRIME MINISTER: Let me raise a final problem, which plagues your society as well as ours. It seems to me that the collapse of communism repudiates the belief—widespread in East and West alike—that vast superstructures of administrative control best promote economic efficiency and technological progress. Our centrally planned economies were justified by claims that organizational giantism would eliminate the "wasteful duplication" and "irrationalities" of the decentral-

[5] See James M. Buchanan, *The Economics and the Ethics of Constitutional Order* (Ann Arbor, Mich.: University of Michigan Press, 1991).

ized, competitive market system—that it would make for a more harmonious, more rational economic order. Clearly, gigantomania failed miserably: The stodgy bureaucracies we built eventually collapsed of their own weight.

But doesn't this problem of bureaucratic bloat and inefficiency afflict private firms as well as state agencies? Whether private corporation in the West, or state ministry in the East, doesn't giantism pose the same threat to economic performance and the standard of living?

ADVISOR: You raise an interesting point. I like the way one of our 1992 presidential candidates, H. Ross Perot, put it. Recalling his frustration with General Motors' bureaucracy after he served on the firm's board of directors, he said: "I come from an environment where, if you see a snake, you kill it. At GM, if you see a snake, the first thing you do is go hire a consultant on snakes. Then you convene a committee on snakes, and you discuss snakes for a couple of years. The most likely outcome is—nothing. You figure, the snake hasn't bitten anybody yet, so you just let it crawl around on the factory floor." (Perot's suggested remedy was to "nuke" the GM bureaucracy.)[6]

PRIME MINISTER: Yet corporate concentration in your country is justified today by the same claims that Lenin and Stalin used decades ago in the Soviet Union— that consolidation and centralization of economic decisionmaking will eliminate "wasteful duplication" and "inefficiency." Isn't such consolidation tantamount to "sovietizing" your own economy? Perhaps you have as

---

6 "The GM System Is Like a Blanket of Fog." *Fortune,* Feb. 15, 1988, 48.

much to learn from us as we do from you. Perhaps the failure of our totalitarian regimes warns of something far more serious than you in the West are willing to admit.[7]

ADVISOR: A key difference, of course, is that your giant organizations were built by government, while our corporations are created by the private sector in the interest of efficiency and profit maximization.

PRIME MINISTER: Your reaction confirms my suspicion that we live in a time when reality conflicts with platitudes, when facts conflict with a priori interpretations—a time of conflict between theory that plays fast and loose with practice and theory that learns from practice.[8]

ADVISOR: It is economic science you criticize.

PRIME MINISTER: No, not science, but humanity's arrogance in an age of science.[9] People's attitude to the world must be radically changed, says Václav Havel: "We have to abandon the arrogant belief that the world is merely a puzzle to be solved, a machine with instructions for use waiting to be discovered, a body of information to be fed into a computer in the hope that, sooner or later, it will spit out a universal solution."[10]

We have to realize that we are locked in a fateful race between the collapse of our inherited institutions and the creation of new ones—that what we are attempting is to convert centuries of backwardness, dictatorship,

[7] See Václav Havel, *Open Letters* (New York: Knopf, 1991), 72, 260.
[8] Ibid., 16.
[9] Ibid., 255. See also William M. Dugger, *Underground Economics: A Decade of Institutionalist Dissent* (Armonk, N.Y.: M. E. Sharpe, 1992).
[10] "The Effort to Exercise Power in Accord with a Vision of Civility," *New York Times*, Jul. 26, 1992, 15A.

corruption, bureaucratic inefficiency, passivity, narrow ethnic nationalism, and a huge chaotic economy into a modern capitalist democracy. It is a task in which new institutions take root only slowly and attitudes are stubbornly impervious to change; a task in which rules are made on the fly; a task that requires us to walk a tightrope toward market democracy, over an abyss of anarchy and terror.

Privatization is not simply a change in ownership; it is a revolution in ways of thinking, acting, and governing.[11] It's a revolutionary answer to the transcending politico-economic questions: Who shall make what economic decisions? On what basis? With what consequences for whom? And with what assurance that the right decisions will be made? Possibilities abound. Options are many. But obstacles cannot be overcome merely by pretending they don't exist. Communism has collapsed, but we don't start from scratch in a vacuum. History—and our institutions, habits, and routines—constrain and limit, but also shape and enable.

Would you agree that what confronts us is as much a social and political challenge as an economic one? That it demands as much bricolage—working with whatever materials are immediately at hand—as it does grand architectural designs drawn up on a tabula rasa? That it requires as much art and agility as it does hardheaded economic science?[12]

ADVISOR: I am aware of all that. Nevertheless, you must

---

[11] For a provocative discussion, see Richard Rose, "Toward a Civil Economy," *Journal of Democracy* 3 (Apr. 1992): 13–26.

[12] See the introduction and articles by David Stark and Peter Murrell *Transforming the Economies of East Central Europe,* special issue of *East European Politics and Societies* 6 (Winter 1992).

begin. And, as the Chinese proverb has it, a thousand-mile journey starts with the first step.

PRIME MINISTER: So it does. But along the way we must be vigilant to protect our freedoms against the forces—public or private—that constantly attempt to erode them. Time has run out for communism. But its concrete edifice still stands. We must, as Aleksandr Solzhenitsyn advised, take care not to be crushed beneath its rubble instead of gaining liberty.[13]

The conference ends. The historic journey continues.

[13] Aleksandr Solzhenitsyn, *Rebuilding Russia* (New York: Farrar, Straus and Giroux, 1991), 3.

Index